The Faceless Statistic

Andrew Michelson

ISBN: 1522789502
ISBN-13: 978-1522789505

ACKNOWLEDGMENTS

I would like that thank various people for their continued support during my time writing this account of my history. Debbie and Jackie for their support in proofing and beta reading. Tony, Shelley, Anita and finally Steve the volunteer on the helpline of R.S.V.P. for your words of support. It's been a tough journey to get through this, but your support and kind words have been gratefully received.

Andrew Michelson

DEDICATION

To all of the faceless statistics out there who suffer alone in silence. There are people who will support and believe you. Be strong and faithful to your beliefs.

Chapter One – Thursday 6th August

As I sat at my computer, I looked through the text of the email once again. Was I really going to send it? Was I finally going to admit what had happened all those years ago? The organisation is dedicated to survivors… but is that what I am? A survivor?

I had never told a soul what happened to me until about four years ago when I came out to the new world that I had set up around me. I was gay. I knew that. I knew it when I was too young to know what it really meant. I hid it for years, from my friends, from my school mates, from my work colleagues and more importantly, from my family.

When I started to come out to the new set of friends that I had, having moved to a new city, I was pointed in the direction of a gay dating site, well; it was more of a hook up site. I felt such a rush of release when I got my first message. A guy, Tony, wanted to meet me. I'd posted on my profile that I was a bottom, a willing submissive, and he was a top. A guy who liked to fuck other guys. We met, we fucked, and we became fuck buddies. We met a few times and a friendship developed between us. He was the first person that I admitted my secret to and he accepted me none the less.

I soon met a second guy, James, as my now blossoming sexuality was released and he took the role plays that I desperately desired to the enth level. He liked playing the role of the dominant top, using my body in ways that I

wanted, that I desired, and I soon told him about my history. It made our meets more intense, more satisfying, more pleasurable. But there was still the emotional connection missing.

I knew that I would never again reach that same level of contentment that I had experienced as a child but I was happy to settle for what I thought was the next best thing.

Life moves on, as it is want to do, and I settled into a nice routine. I had a good job, a family who lived far enough away that they didn't know about my true life but close enough that I see them once a fortnight, and a great set of new friends who accepted me for the 'great guy' that I am. I had enough contacts through the hook up site that I could almost get sex on tap. Did I need anything else?

I guess that I did.

Four years later, a new group friendship of fellow budding authors opened my eyes to what happened to me all those years ago. That chance comment to one of the group members who had suffered her own sexual abuse led me into a conversation that I never thought that I'd have with a woman, well, with anyone outside of my bedroom. It led to thoughts and memories that, when revisited, could change the very foundations of what my life has been built on.

This is my story.

It might not sit right with some. It might find a common link with others. Some people who have never been in my situation will claim that I could not ever feel the way that I did. Others who will always remain silent will never admit that they felt the same way that I did. That is the way of our world. Demonise those that we cannot understand, while standing on our own fake righteousness as we fail to see what is happening all around us.

Recent studies suggest that one child in twenty in the United Kingdom is currently being sexually abused. I believe that the figure for boys is that one in six will have been sexually abused by the time he turns sixteen, the now legal age of consent for both hetero and homosexual contact. This is backed up with several scientific studies in the USA. One in three children sexually abused by an adult will not tell about their abuse, mainly due to ninety percent of child sexual abusers being known to that child. Cajoled into secrecy with promises of gifts, threats of how the child will be in trouble or simply being told that it was how people showed their love to each other, buys the abuser their silence.

I am one of those percentages, one of those statistics. I never told. I never wanted to because of how I was brought up to believe about what had happened to me. I was one of those faceless statistics… until now.

This is my story.

This is how I remember my life, growing up. As I revisit my memories and work through my experiences, I have decided to chronicle my growing understanding and recollections of what happened to me, how I felt at the time, how it has shaped my life and how I feel now that I am talking about it. I will not mince my words and I will tell it exactly how I remember and how I believed I felt.

This is my story.

Andrew Michelson

Chapter Two – The Innocence of Youth

I was born into a working class, two parent two child family, with a sister who was older than me by nearly three years. One of my earliest recollections was of the public house that my Great Aunt and Uncle ran, which we visited regularly. They had a lovely black dog, I'm not sure of the breed, but the name I will always remember for the pure, now un-political correctness of it. Blackie! My sister and I, along with my Great Aunt, used to take it for walks around the town where they lived, and I never felt any shame in shouting for "Blackie" to come back when he was off the leash. There simply weren't that many black people around in those days, and even if there was, it didn't seem to carry the same connotation that it does now.

Those days? In those days we had three television channels and a remote control that consisted of getting up off your backside to change the channel by pressing the selector on the set. No Playstations or X Boxes… Space Invaders was the highest level of gaming technology, and that was mainly only in arcades. Our games were outside games. We had no fear of playing outside. Summer holidays were spent roaming woods, making forts, playing football in the fields and making sure that you were home before dark otherwise the imprint of mother's hand would be seen in red on the back of your legs.

Holidays were always a fun time with my family. Despite my sister being nearly three years older than me, and that

we sometimes fought like cat and mouse, we still hung out and played when it was just the two of us. A relative had a house down in North Devon which we went to sometimes, or a caravan park at the seaside.

I never realised until years later that we were fortunate to go on the holidays, my parents scrimping and saving up to make sure we didn't miss out. They told me, after my own descent into debt a few years ago, about how they used to fear an unexpected knock on the front door, wondering if this one would be a debt collector or a bailiff.

So it was with some relief for them that each year, my Great Aunt, my Nan and a female friend of my Aunt's would take my sister and me on holiday with them. It was always to the same place, a Pontins holiday camp down south. If I remember rightly, it was Minehead. The chalets were quite cramped and I normally ended up in a bunk bed, arguing with my sister as to who got the top bunk. She would always win after giving me a Chinese burn to submit! We would go off with the Bluecoats, the park staff who had children's activities organised, leaving my older female relatives free to relax, play bingo and idly chat with other ladies of their age.

All in all, life was innocently good. I wasn't the sportiest lad at school, but I was a good cross country runner, similar to my sister who ran for an athletics club in the city. I had a good set of friends, and attracted the interest of girls within my class. I had an all year long tan, I guess from being outside whenever possible, and my platinum blonde hair only started to darken when I was about ten or eleven. Looking back, without any hint of vanity, I would say that I was a good looking kid.

I was also a friendly young boy, having no trouble making friends either at school, or at Cubs, where I became the Sixer of my pack. I still look back at pictures of me, dressed in my green Cub shirt, blue and red neckerchief with my grey toggle and wonder about my

innocence. With an arm full of merit badges, I loved the experiences of being around boys.

And so, it was with a lot of naivety that my first unwanted sexual experience happened at the tender age of eight years old. I just didn't realise it at the time. Remember, this was a time before the stranger danger campaigns and the high profile abuse cases so I was an innocent boy with no idea that my willy could be used for anything other than peeing. Hindsight, however, is a wonderful or regretful thing.

My sister had followed my mother into being a Brownie, and then a Girl Guide, and had gone off to camp when it came to the annual holiday with my elder female relatives. Always happy to be going on holiday, even if it was just myself with my Nan, Great Aunt and their friend, I was confident that I would make friends easily. I was a happy go lucky kid, rarely getting into fights and was excited that I would finally get to sleep on the top bunk.

We checked in as normal and the routine easily settled into the habits of previous holidays. My elder female relatives would wake me for breakfast, we'd eat in the huge dining hall before I bade them farewell until lunch. We'd meet outside the dining hall and I would enthusiastically explain what I had been doing all morning before heading off for an afternoon full of fun. Dinner was eaten and we stayed in the main hall for the evening's entertainment which, if you ever watched the television series Hi-De-Hi, was exactly like that! Poor comedians, ballroom dancing and music from the Sixties, despite this being the early Eighties. Oh, how I hated being forced onto the dance floor to be paraded around by the three women.

Looking back now, the very first inkling that I should have had that I was a boy attracting the wrong kind of attention was on the third morning that we were there. As it was the age long before mobile phones became available to all and sundry, my Great Aunt wanted to use the public telephone to ring my Great Uncle to ensure that the pub

was still standing, and she suggested that I rang home to speak to my parents. I did so and afterwards, while I sat down on the row of plastic chairs waiting for my Great Aunt to make her call, I didn't really pay any attention to the two men who came to sit either side of me. It was fairly busy so I'd just assumed that they sat where they could. They were old, to me anyway, but I am guessing now that they were probably in their late twenties or early thirties. I cannot remember all the details of the conversation that they struck up with me, but I do remember telling them that I was one of the best runners in the school. The one on my left told me to straighten my leg so that he could see the muscles and I willingly obliged. After all, we were brought up respecting our elders. He proceeded to run his hand up and down my leg, starting at my knee but stopping just before his fingers reached my shorts. He told me that my muscles were getting big.

His friend asked me if he could check my muscles on my right leg and I told him that it should be better as I was right footed at football. He was soon repeating the actions of his friend. I looked over at my Great Aunt who was glancing in my direction, something that one of the men noticed. He asked me if I was with her, to which I replied in the positive, and before I knew what had happened, I was sitting alone once more. My Great Aunt never mentioned it or warned me about the perils of letting men that I didn't know touch my body, so I never thought that it was wrong. I thought that it was simply two friendly men wanting to compliment me on how my muscles were developing.

That day passed as the others had and it was with three days to go that I was first touched inappropriately. With the weather in the UK being like it was, a rainy day meant indoor fun. I decided that I wanted to go swimming, something that my elderly female relatives certainly had no intention of doing. After my Nan had checked with me

that I knew where the swimming pool was, I headed out into the rain, dressed in shorts, a t-shirt and a hat to keep the rain off. With my swimming trunks already on, I had a pair of underpants tucked away in my rolled up towel as I ran halfway across the camp to the indoor pool.

I was nervously excited as, despite being able to swim for a number of years, I had recently learned how to dive properly. Being a member of my local swimming club, that was paramount to me being able to start representing them in competitions.

I got to the pool and it was packed. It seemed like every family had had the same idea as me for keeping dry... by jumping into a pool full of water! I quickly ran into the male changing room and found an empty locker. Stripping out of my t-shirt and shorts, I threw everything inside and locked it, slipping the rubber band which held the key around my ankle, just as I had been taught back home. My main mischievousness as a boy was that I hated walking through the chlorine footbath and so I jumped over it, making sure that the lifeguard wasn't watching.

Little did I know at that time that someone else was, someone who took an interest in me as soon as he realised that I was at the pool alone. I jumped in and quickly swam a few lengths to warm up from the shock of the coldness of the water before slowing down and hanging on the edge of the pool to look around. I wanted to find some boys my own age that I could play with, tag or something similar, but I only saw girls and older boys. I knew from my experiences back home that teenage boys did not want eight year olds hanging around with them, especially if there were girls around... something that I still didn't understand why. After all, most girls were rubbish at football!

"You look like a good swimmer," a soft voice said from behind me, making me jump and swallow a mouthful of water. I felt his hand pat me on the back as I coughed and spluttered it back up.

"Thank you, sir," I finally was able to reply. I didn't take much notice that he continued to rub my back.

"Call me Barry," he told me and held out a hand. I looked at it surprised. Adults didn't shake hands with kids, did they? I took it, thinking that he must think I was older than I was and told him that my name was "Andrew. Not Andy. Andrew."

"I have a son that must be about your age," Barry started. "He's ten."

"I'm eight!" I replied.

"You look a little older," he smiled, making me feel good. I wasn't the smallest in my class but there were quite a few boys who were taller than me.

"Where is he? What's his name?" I asked, looking around, hoping for a play mate.

"Danny couldn't make it," Barry sighed. "He lives with his mummy and she wanted him to stay at home."

That confused me as I'd never heard of a mummy and daddy living apart and he quickly explained that they had fallen out of love and he had moved away. I scrunched my nose up at the L word, something which he laughed at. He challenged me to a race and, with the lack of anyone my age to play with, I accepted. We swam a couple of lengths and I beat him… just. Of course, I didn't know that he had let me win but as he stroked my shoulder, telling me how good a swimmer I was, my self-confidence grew in leaps and bounds. I challenged him to a proper race, one where we started off on the side and dived in. After all, I wanted to show off my new skill.

"What do you mean you can't dive?" I gasped as he told me that he didn't know how.

"I was never shown how so I tend to just fall in the water, belly first," he told me, making me giggle at the image in my head.

"I can show you how!" I told him and pulled myself up out of the pool. I looked back to see him staring at me but thought nothing of it. I held out a hand to help him out of

the pool, which he took. I was surprised that he didn't pull me back in, something that I did a lot to my friends, but as he stood on the side of the pool next to me, I concentrated on explaining where to put his feet, curling his toes around the curved edge.

"You better show me," he said, and I stood next to him, curling mine around.

"Now, you bend over like you are going to touch your toes but put your hands out in front of you," I explained.

He made a poor effort and I realised that I would have to show him. As soon as I was in position, he moved his body so that he was stood behind me. He crouched himself over my body, telling me that he wanted to use me as a model for how to hold his own body. That sounded very reasonable and sensible to me. I didn't fail to notice his groin pushing into my backside though, something that sent a tingle through me for some reason. As soon as he was leaning over me and his hands had released mine, I said "now dive" and pushed off and dove into the pool. He belly flopped in, a loud crack of flesh on water as he smacked the surface, causing me to burst into a fit of laughter.

"You didn't do it right," I told him and dragged him to the side of the pool. We pulled ourselves out of the water and once again, I got into the correct position. He repeated his action of leaning over me, holding me as he "got himself into the correct position" and we tried again. And again. And again. Each time I felt him pushing something into the back of my swimming trunks and it made me confused. I was nowhere near puberty at that point and sex was definitely not a topic of conversation with my parents so I didn't understand what was happening. However, it did feel nice when he wrapped his arms around my wet body as he got into the correct diving position.

Finally, he got it right and we raced each other until I began to tire. That's when I noticed that I was late. I

hadn't kept my eye on the big clock, with its slow moving second hand and large minute and hour hands. It was ten minutes past when I should have been back at the chalet and I started to panic.

"What's wrong, honey?" Barry asked, and as I explained I had to go and that I was late already, I could feel the tears beginning to well up in my eyes. "Come on, don't cry." He put his arm around me and held me. "Let's both get out and I'll help you shower and get you back as quickly as you can."

I thanked him for his kindness and we quickly scrambled out of the pool. I ran to my locker, pulling my towel out, dropping my underpants onto the wet floor. It seemed that everything wanted to go against me. I pushed them back into the locker before closing it and turning to face the man whom I thought was my saviour. He motioned for me to go into one of the shower stalls and he followed me in, closing the door behind him. He put a bar of soap on the shelf and flicked the lid from a bottle of shampoo.

He turned the tap on, adjusting the freezing cold flow of water until it was just right and he positioned me underneath it, re-wetting my hair. He poured some shampoo into his hands and quickly lathered up my hair. I revelled in the feel of his hands massaging my head gently but had to keep my eyes closed to stop the soapy suds from stinging them. I felt him stop but he told me to keep my eyes closed while he put on a second helping of shampoo. His hands returned to my head, rubbing his fingers through my blonde locks and I must have let out a sigh of satisfaction as he asked me if I was enjoying it.

After telling him yes, he rinsed my hair before grabbing the soap from the shelf. He lathered his hands up before beginning to wash my chest and arms. I giggled as he tickled underneath my arms before IT happened. Having got use to his touch, I didn't complain as his hands worked lower onto my stomach before he reached for my swimming trunks. Being the naïve eight year old, I didn't

think that there was anything wrong with a responsible, caring adult taking the time to help me so I just stood there and let him remove my trunks. I clearly remember giggling as I kicked them into the corner before watching as he lathered his hands up again.

He took a deep breath, not saying a word as he lowered his hands to my body once more. He washed me thoroughly which, to my surprise, made my little willy react by getting stiff but before I could say anything, he washed my backside as well. I felt a little uncomfortable when he washed in-between my cheeks but he simply whispered that I needed to be clean everywhere. I do remember him touching my hole but don't recall him actually penetrating me with his finger so I am guessing that he was testing the water, so to speak.

He positioned me back under the stream of the shower and used his hands to wash off the suds before he said that it was his turn to get clean. As he peeled off his own swimming trunks, I couldn't help but see his willy, which was standing upright. I thought that there might be something wrong with it so I didn't say anything. He offered me the soap to help clean him but I told him that it would be quicker if he washed himself. My mind was on the ticking clock and the clip around the ear that I was going to get if I was too much longer.

He sighed and washed himself, spending a long time washing his willy. It looked strange to me, how he washed it. I generally just rubbed quickly with the flannel but he seemed to be cleaning the length of it over and over again. His breathing got faster until he suddenly made a funny sound. Some white stuff shot out the end of his willy and hit me in the chest. I screwed up my nose, thinking that he had peed on me, but then the sound of several other people coming into the shower area made him cover my mouth with his hand to quiet my questions. He looked around over the door to the stall and quickly rinsed me and himself under the stream of water.

Grabbing our towels, he led me back out into the changing room, whispering to me that I should call him "Uncle Barry" if anyone asked. I just shrugged as I had several friends of my parents and of my Nan whom I called Aunt and Uncle, even though they weren't related to me.

He dried me, again spending a little longer than probably he should have in a certain area of my groin, but all in all, I was a clean little boy who quickly dressed and said goodbye to my new friend. I ran back to the chalet, getting scolded for being late and we went off for dinner.

Looking back with my adult hindsight, I had been molested by Barry, who had seen the opportunity to get a boy naked to play with. I think that if I had gone back swimming the next day, it would probably have happened again, and maybe the start of a short grooming process that could possibly have ended up with more than just touching and him masturbating over me. After all, he had wanted me to touch him so who knows where it would have led. However, the next day was a sunny day so I wanted to play outside and met up with the Bluecoats who had a full day's activities planned for us kids. I didn't see him again for the remainder of the holiday.

My over-riding memory as a child of that holiday wasn't the encounter with the two men at the telephone booths, or even the shower with Barry, but it was the loss of my beloved Star Wars collector cards that I remembered the most. I had collected nearly the complete set, taking them with me wherever I went, and at night, I used to look at them as they told the story of the film. As I was on the top bunk, I used to place them on the ridge of the curtain rail when I went to sleep and it was only when we were half way home, some three hundred miles when I realised that I had left them on the curtain shelf. I cried for days, or at least until my parents bought me a new football anyway.

It was in the last year of primary school, while I was ten going on eleven, when the strangest emotion started. I was on my third or fourth girlfriend of the school year, which mainly involved hanging around with her and her friends at break and lunch times rather than playing football with my mates. There was a lot of hand holding and kisses were just pecks on the lips as we were too young to know about French kissing. Sex education wasn't until middle school!

I can remember sitting with Carole, trying to pretend that I wasn't jealous watching my mates and the other lads of year four playing football against the year three boys. My eyes were drawn to a lad from year three that I couldn't remember seeing before. His blonde hair was cut short around his ears and just above his shoulders and he had a face of an angel. His cheeks were slightly puffed out, as though he had constantly taken in a deep breath, and his body was slim.

I felt my stomach stirring, despite having eaten my lunch, and a strange feeling in my groin. Without knowing what it was or why it had occurred, I had experienced my first true erection of my pre-pubescent life. I became infatuated with the boy, Matthew, as I discovered his name was. From never noticing him in school before, I now saw him constantly, my eyes scanning the crowded dining room or assembly hall, looking for just a sneaked glimpse of him.

Carole soon noticed that I wasn't paying her enough attention and after a brief argument, I dumped her so that I could go back to playing football, and maybe get closer to my new obsession. I wasn't the best footballer in the world, despite my dreams of playing for my beloved Leicester City, but I was a quick runner and could kick the ball to my team mates, most of the time anyway. Despite being on the same pitch as him, there wasn't any real interaction that I could muster. Off the pitch, of course, it

wasn't the done thing, associating with anyone from the year below unless it was a sibling. So I watched him from afar, not saying anything to anyone. It actually turned out, when I bumped into him years later in a pub, that he was a bit of an arrogant git so I am pleased that nothing actually occurred between us.

At home, I became a little withdrawn when it came to the subject of girls. I remember being very confused when I watched a film with my family. It was called "The Orphan Train" and was about these homeless kids from New York who get loaded onto a train and it went across America, stopping at various towns and cities. The idea was that the adults who had organised it were trying to get them adopted. There was one character called JP, a scamp of a lad with blonde hair who wasn't quite as tough as the other boys. He did get into a fight but cried when he got a bloodied nose, which one of the male adults tried to tell him to toughen up. I found myself very attracted to him, being around my age or slightly older and I shifted several times on the sofa to hide my growing erection. The confusion for me was mainly that it was discovered that JP was actually Josephine Priscilla. The girl had disguised herself as a boy to get work while she was in New York and had carried it through to the journey. When she was eventually clothed in a dress, I didn't find her very appealing at all and it was then that I began to realise that I preferred looking at boys rather than girls.

This completely changed my outlook at school and at play with my mates. With swimming lessons at school and my membership of the swimming club, I had ample opportunities to look at other boys in various states of undress. I began secretly comparing myself to them, but was embarrassed that I seemed to be smaller than most in the penis department. Some of my friends filled their swimming trunks and underpants quite nicely whereas I seemed to have just the smallest lump. It was this that led to my first, real, sexual education lesson.

One Saturday morning, I had gone swimming with my friend Simon. We weren't best friends, and I seem to remember that he didn't really seem to have many friends at all. His parents were fairly well off and seemed quite snobby, at least from my young perspective but Simon and I were the only two boys of our age who were in the church choir. This lead to us becoming friends as again, the older boys didn't really have a lot of time for us and we certainly weren't talking to the girls! We had messed around for a couple of hours, avoiding the lifeguard when it came to our time being up before we finally grew tired and decided to get out.

The showers in our club were open so no-one ever showered naked. After washing the chlorine from our bodies, we headed back into the changing room. There were private stalls if you wanted to go in for modesty but, being boys, we got changed next to our lockers. As he peeled him trunks off, I quickly grabbed myself a sneaky look at his goods. Again, my heart sank a little as he looked to be twice the size of me. I draped my towel over my shoulder, ready for my usual trick of dropping my trunks and quickly wrapping the towel around my waist so that my little piece of embarrassment wouldn't get seen. However, as I took my trunks down, Simon grabbed my towel and twisted it quickly and snapped it at my bum. It stung like mad but as I tried to get out of the way of his follow up snaps while trying to grab the towel at the same time, I was fully exposed to him.

"Do you play with it yet?" he asked me as he suddenly stopped hitting me with my towel.

"Huh?" I was a bright lad, but not about matters yet to be discussed.

"Your dick. It's a bit small," he said, but not in a teasing manner. He pushed his hips forward, showing me his willy. It was limp, hanging down, and looked to be about two inches long. It was quite thin still, just like mine.

"I know mine's small," I huffed. "It's not fair… I just want a big one like the others."

"Well, you have to exercise it," he explained.

"How?"

"Like this." He proceeded to take his willy in his hand and pulled the skin back. He repeated the actions of Barry, and I realised that the exercise must make your willy grow really big. Even as I watched Simon, his willy started getting bigger in front of my eyes.

"Wow!" I said and started to follow his actions on my own, small willy. It immediately grew longer and got really hard. However, before I could exercise it any more, some other boys came into the changing room so we stopped and quickly got dressed, just in case the older boys were looking for smaller kids to pick on.

We ran back to his house and escaped his parents' attention by going to his room. I asked him how he knew about the exercise and he told me that his dad had given him the talk. I looked at him perplexed and he giggled and told me that if I wanted to feel really good, then I should do the exercise until I get the feeling.

That night, desperate to make my willy grow bigger, I exercised it right up to the point where I thought I was going to pee myself. I ran to the bathroom but nothing came out. This happened several times before I realised that it must be the 'feeling' that Simon had told me about. The next time, I didn't stop and my whole body shook as I experienced my first dry orgasm. I fell asleep straight away, my pyjama bottoms around my ankles and my blanket to the side. Why my parents didn't say anything to me I have no idea. At least one of them must have known that I was becoming a man because I woke up the next morning with my pyjama bottoms in place and my covers pulled over me.

I couldn't wait to tell Simon about it, but as he went to the other school in our town, I had to wait until choir

practice. He just smiled at me and said, "it's great, isn't it?" Who was I to argue?

However, no matter how much I exercised it, my development was slow and I remained smaller than most of my friends and, with my parents still failing to explain about the birds and the bees, I was left alone to my experimentation. This took a new turn one cold Saturday evening after an accidental viewing of what, to my young mind, was hardcore pornography. Saturday evenings were always the same. My parents would be sitting on the three seater settee while my sister and I would take an armchair each. The Generation Game and Blankety Blank would take up the early evening entertainment before other boring adult programmes ticked away the time until Match of the Day came on. As a mad football fan, I couldn't wait for the weekly highlights show when I could watch my heroes. My sister didn't care for football but as the alternative was to go to bed, she stayed silent as my parents snored through the programme. The end credits always seemed to wake them up, much like an alarm clock, and the end of the programme meant bedtime. I'd started to get quite sneaky though and, as the league table was shown, I'd quietly creep to the television and turn the sound down. This kept my parents asleep and allowed us kids to have extra time before we were sent to bed.

Normally there would be a late night film, some horror which I hated but my sister loved. This particular night however, there was a film starring Joan Collins, whom I recognised from watching Dynasty. My eyes boggled as she was soon naked, her breasts bouncing as she had sex with some bloke. The film was either The Stud or The Bitch but then my parents woke up and we were dismissed to bed rather quickly. My mind was full of the images that I had seen on screen, especially where the man had been on top of her, but despite seeing more of Joan Collins than

the man, it was still the man that I remembered looking at more.

School ticked along as it always did, but with winter drawing in, our outside play was curtailed and we were forced indoors. Whilst not at the top of the popularity list, I did have a good number of friends so it wasn't a problem to keep myself occupied. I was so jealous of one of my friends, Paul, whose parents had bought him an Atari console. Fortunately, because his mother and mine were good friends, we had been 'forced' into playing together from an early age. I spent many afternoons after school and weekends around his house, playing Frogger or Space Invaders. There was another lad, Dave, who usually hung around with us, but to be honest, we didn't really get along. He was a bigger, stronger lad than me and a bit of a bully, and whenever we played football, I always came home with multiple bruises where he had kicked me. I used to hate it whenever he was around, but put up with him for the sake of my friendship with Paul, which was a confusing one. I had begun to recognise that I was developing crushes on some of the boys at school, and their older brothers, but Paul never seemed to be in my thoughts when it came to things like that. The three of us used to wrestle, more at the insistence of Dave than Paul, which I think was more so that he could overpower me and show me how much weaker I was compared to him. One evening, when Dave had not been allowed to come around, Paul instigated a rough and tumble wrestle in his room. For once, I enjoyed myself as I could just about hold my own against a boy closer to my own height and weight, but I was still a little shocked when he grabbed me in a certain place. He'd stammered out an apology but I just grinned and pounced on him, pinning him to the ground. I held his shoulders down and counted to three, in true wrestling style, before sitting back up, my legs either side of his waist. I felt that he'd gotten hard and I giggled as he squirmed underneath me, trying to throw me

off him, which he eventually did. That's when he asked if I wanted to play the rape game.

"Rape game?" I asked, perplexed. I had no idea what the word meant, or what the game actually was.

"Yeah... it's really cool," Paul babbled excitedly. "Stay there!" He dashed out of his bedroom, reappearing moments later with one of his sister's cuddly toys.

"What do we do?" I asked again, wanting to know what this really cool game could be.

"Shove this up your tee-shirt so that it looks like you've got boobies," he told me, handing me the teddy bear.

"Why?"

"Cos it's part of the game, dummy!"

Not wanting to be caught looking like I was stupid, I followed his instruction and he stood me in front of his mirror. He went to his closet and rummaged around at the bottom of it before pulling out a blonde wig. "Put this on."

"No way!" I hissed. "I'll look like a girl!"

"That's the idea, dummy!"

"But..." I started to argue. Although I knew that I now liked to look at boys more than girls, I was still a boy myself. I hadn't really heard of being gay, or what it actually meant back then.

"Look, you play the girl first and then I'll be the girl," Paul explained. With that counter offer in mind, I happily donned the wig.

Cutting a long story short, the basis of the game was that I "walked past" him all innocently and he would grab me from behind and grope my "boobies". We would then swap roles and I would do the same to him. I didn't really get it, but remembering back to how the man had touched Joan Collins, I tried my best.

It all seemed silly to me, but I could tell that my mate was into it so I happily played along for the next couple of times. I had no idea about the actual connotation of what

we were doing, in terms of practicing to "rape" someone, as to me, it was just about groping the "boobies".

However, it turned into a different game the first time that Paul got the teddy and the wig when Dave was there. As mentioned, while Dave and I hung out together with Paul, we would never hang out when it was just the two of us. We never went to each others' houses on our own as we didn't really get along. Dave would take every opportunity that he could to show that he was stronger than me and suddenly, the idea of dressing up and pretending to be a girl while he was there didn't sound like fun.

Paul insisted though, and as he was my best mate at the time, I didn't want to fall out with him. So I put the wig on and pushed the teddy bear up my t-shirt and began my slow walk around Paul's bedroom. Sure enough, Paul grabbed me and pushed me onto his bed falling on top of me, feeling up my fake boobies, just like normal. When he had finished, I started to take the wig off to give to either of them when Dave said it was his turn to be the grabber. I offered Paul the wig but he said that we would all take it in turns letting the other two go be the grabber before swapping. That sounded fair to my mind, but I couldn't help but feel uncomfortable as I willingly allowed the stronger boy to grab me from behind and push me onto Paul's bed. His body landed on top of me and his arms had encircled my chest. As he started to squeeze and rub the teddy bear in what I imagine his idea of fondling a woman would be, he also started to grind his hips into me. His groin was pressed into my denim jean covered bottom but I could still feel it poking against me and I realised that his willy had gotten hard. The thought ran through my mind that he must have been exercising it a lot because it felt a lot bigger than mine, and it was just another knock of my self-confidence. I struggled to try to get out from underneath him but he just held me tighter and told me not to fight it or he'd thump me. As he continued his

humping, I felt my own little willy grow hard as the friction of being pushed into Paul's bed made itself known. I started to gasp and fight against him but he was too strong and suddenly he let out a sigh and just sort of flopped onto me. I pushed him off of me and threw the wig away while taking the teddy bear out of my shirt. My willy was so hard that I was almost doubled up as I stood up and I ran from the room, not wanting them to see me. I locked myself in the toilet and splashed water on my face until my willy returned to normal and I excused myself from the house, running home and going straight into my room. My parents were used to the fights that Dave and I got into sometimes so this was nothing new, they just left me alone with a warning to go to bed at my normal time as it was a school night.

I laid on my bed, my thoughts swirling at the feelings that I had felt while Dave was on top of me, holding me down. As much as I didn't like him and no way in the world would ever fantasise about him, the feelings that he gave me were indescribable. When I went to bed that night, instead of my usual willy exercise, I rolled myself onto my front and tried to re-enact the feeling but to no avail. Without someone pushing me down, I just couldn't get the friction. Obviously I couldn't go and ask my parents or my sister, so my mind quickly devised an alternative. Rolling up one of my pillows, I slipped it underneath me, raising my groin and stomach from the bed. My body weight now pressed down on my raised mid-section and I found that I easily replicated the friction that got my willy so hard before.

Ever since that day, even throughout my adult life, my favourite solo form of masturbation has remained unchanged, with only the addition of a sock to prevent me having to continually wash the pillow.

Andrew Michelson

Chapter Three – Wednesday 18th August

My email pinged, as it is want to do, and I quickly discarded the numerous junk emails and the book promotion emails that I had signed up for. It had been nearly two weeks since I pressed send on THAT email and I'd heard nothing back so, with a feeling of being pissed off as I'd finally had the courage to reach out to someone, only for nothing to have happened, I had fired off a sarcastic email "thanking" them for their reply.

Of course, this prompted a reply from a lady who said that she had been on holiday and apologised for the delay. She gave me details of a charity for rape and sexual violence victims based in my area. Suddenly, I was faced with those awful words. Rape. Violence. Victim.

Was that what I was? A victim of violent rape. I didn't think so. I have spent the whole of my adult life living with the assumptions that I wasn't raped or abused, that I had been a willing, submissive participant but again, the words of my fellow author came back to haunt me. "The bastards", as she called them, didn't deserve to get away with what they had done to us, to others and it got me thinking once more.

Guilt reared its head as I remembered feeling the anger pour from her that first time that we spoke, anger that I just didn't feel. I struggled to understand how we could have gone through similar experiences yet have such a

vastly different outlook on it, and so I began to doubt my own memories.

For days I toyed with ringing the telephone number. I spoke with Tony at some length over text messages, about my mixed feelings and he told me not to feel guilty, that it wasn't my fault. Instead of focussing on feeling bad, I should concentrate on what I now enjoy doing. This prompted a long sexting session which the pair of us ended up masturbating to. Of course, as a submissive bottom, I had to use a toy on myself to get the maximum feeling of pleasure, but it worked. I guess that the rush of pheromones that course through your body after an orgasm makes the world feel like such a better place.

Deciding to have the courage, via a couple of pints of lager, I rang the helpline, only for it to be after hours. I left a brief message, giving my mobile number and explaining very briefly that I had been sexually active as a child, but now was having some mixed emotions and wanted to talk.

I took a phone call at work and found out that the helpline had a male volunteer on a Tuesday evening and Saturday morning and I said that would be fine.

I carried on with life for the next few days, not really thinking about it, concentrating on the other book which I am writing, and watching the numerous television series that I had recorded when suddenly my phone rang. Not recognising the number, I answered cautiously to discover that it was the male volunteer ringing me as my details were in their system. I panicked, suddenly not ready to face the conversation and told him that I wasn't ready to talk. He was fine with that and left it that I would call him when I was ready.

Panic over! So I decided to continue exploring my memories, trying to find out whether my recollections were correct, or if there was stuff that I had blocked. For instance, it was only looking back that I realised that Barry had touched me at a younger age than I had originally

thought. I had believed it had happened when I was ten years old but the recollection of losing my beloved Star Wars cards led me to realise that it had happened two years before. So what else of my memories were blurred or fudged by my desire not to have been a victim?

I also started to have concerns about how much detail I should go into about my experiences. How much do I want to make public? Most people who know me will never know about this book. They will never read it. They will never know about the experiences that I went through. But some will. Tony will read it. My friend in the writers group will read it. I will need to get this edited so that will be another person who knows me who will read it. What will they think of me if I put everything in… but at the same time, is it worth writing if I don't?

I suppose this is the problem with writing your own story. My story.

Andrew Michelson

Chapter Four – A Summer of Play and Discovery

The last day of a school year was always a fun time, but with it being the last day at our Primary school, it was a little more special, a little sadder but also exciting that we were going to the "big" school. The big school as my parents called it, was actually the middle school, even though it was called the "High School". It was where we would stay for the next three years, from the age of eleven to fourteen before we moved on to the Grammar School to spend the two years of our GCE's and O'Levels.

I knew that we would be sharing the school with our arch rival primary school from across town, as well as some of the local village schools but that was for another day. We had eight weeks of summer holidays and I intended to enjoy them as best as I could.

As usual, I spent most of it down the field with Paul and Dave playing football, and with the weather being great throughout, there was no need for us to be at anyone's house. This allowed me to escape any repeat of the rape game, and the confusing feelings that I had experienced when Dave had been on top of me.

Trees were climbed, footballs kicked and the old junkyard of the foundry works explored. Despite the television series finishing, Blake's Seven was still one of our favourite role playing games. We fought and hid from the evil Space Federation, using sticks as guns and broken bricks as

grenades, and the old junkyard was a perfect setting for the games. Of course, we had been warned on several occasions to stay out of the foundry yard but, being eleven, we knew better than the spoilsport adults. Was it any surprise that Paul ended up at the hospital to have stitches put in the six inch cut on his leg after he slipped and sliced it open on a sharp piece of metal?

My Dad also started to take me down to the local working men's club. It was basically a pub, but one that you needed to be a member of to get in. As the son of a member, I was allowed in as they didn't have a children's membership scheme, and soon, every Sunday lunchtime, I was racing home from church to go to the pub! Not bad for an eleven year old.

The main attraction for me was the pool table. There were a group of boys, whose ages ranged from a couple of years younger than me to about three years older than me. I recognised one of the boys as being in the same school year as my sister. We played pool, and even had competitions organised by one of the club's committee members and I turned out to be a decent player. I had a growing collection of trophies to my name and a new interest outside of Paul and Dave, who didn't come as their Dad's weren't members. I desperately wanted my own cue, something that Santa brought me that Christmas.

Despite being a cub scout, I did miss out on going to camps because, to my embarrassment, I had a problem with bedwetting until I was nine. It stopped just as I moved on to scouts, but I didn't really like Scouts so left soon after joining. I loved camping out in a tent and, during the good weather, my sister and I would put up the two man tent in our back garden and camp out. She was nearly three years older than me, but despite being a girl, she was very sporty so we did have some things in common. I had hidden it from my parents, but I did like to read her magazines and annuals such as Jackie and Bunty, so we talked about the stories in them as well.

Being confused about my feelings towards my male friends, I still tried to like girls as I didn't want to seem weird or strange. My Dad was a mechanic for a big manufacturing company and all of his friends were of a similar ilk. All of them were macho men and being homosexual just wasn't a done thing. While he had never come out as being gay, Larry Grayson who presented the Generation Game was the epitome of campness, and my Dad use to make a lot of derogatory remarks about him, so I kept my mouth shut about being attracted to men and boys.

It was during this summer that I saw my first naked girl and got my first proper French kiss. While I had had a string of girlfriends at Primary school, the kisses were just pecks on lips. My sister had some friends who used to have sleepovers and, despite my attraction to the males of the species, I really fancied Rachel, one of the regular sleepover friends. I think my sister knew as she would always try to get the pair of them to walk into my room as I was getting undressed for bed. Of course, I would get totally embarrassed at being caught in just my underwear by the thirteen and fourteen year old girls who would just giggle at me trying to hide my body. Nothing ever happened between Rachel and myself, much to my disappointment, but it was the set up for what would happen next.

It was one hot summer's day when my sister persuaded my parents to let us put the tent up in the garden so that we could camp out. My Dad was a proud gardener and I remember that he didn't let us have the tent up for more than a couple of days at a time as it ruined the grass. I don't know why he was so proud of the garden as I used to destroy it on a regular basis, not on purpose of course, but when I played football in the garden, sometimes the ball would hit the flowers and they'd explode in a firework display of petals.

As it was a hot day, my sister had also spread a blanket out on the grass and was sunbathing in her bikini. While she was quite tall, she was also slim and toned due to her athletic commitments, which without being nasty or rude, meant that she was also fairly flat chested. As the tent was up and the blanket on the ground, this meant that there was hardly any room for me to kick my football about on the lawn. We did have a paved area directly outside the kitchen and the patio door leading into the dining room, but experience had taught me that I couldn't keep the my shots below window height and I certainly didn't want to feel my mother's hand slapping against the back of my leg. It hurt far too much, so I settled down on the blanket next to her. I was shirtless, as normal, dressed just in my shorts and trainers and, with lack of anything to do, I kicked them off as well so that I could work on my tan.

Evening came around and we'd eaten tea before being told to get washed and get ready for bed. Why we had to have a wash just to go to bed I never knew, but being the obedient boy, I went into the bathroom, ran the tap, splashed the water around in the basin and came back out. I got into my t-shirt and underpants that I wore to bed, and headed back outside to the tent. I was sat on top of my sleeping bag when my sister arrived, laden down with snacks for our midnight feast. Dad zipped up the tent, warning us not to make too much noise before scaring the crap out of us by coming back a few minutes later to make monster noises outside the tent!

We settled down, reading comics and magazines when my sister showed me the latest story that we both followed in one of hers. I think it was called the Four Marys and was about a boarding school with four girls called Mary, obviously. They would have various adventures but this particular one had one of the Mary's falling in love with a visiting prince. There were a couple of pictures of them kissing before he had to go back to whatever country he was from and the story ended.

It was quite late and I am sure that my parents must have gone to bed already, probably enjoying a night free from us being in the house. That was when my sister asked me if I'd ever kissed anyone.

"Of course I have," I replied, indignant that she thought I wouldn't have.

"Who?" she asked, and I quickly listed the four girls, Carole, Rebecca from when I was in year two, and two more whose names now slip my mind.

"I don't believe you," she said.

"How can I prove it?" I asked. "I mean, I don't go out with them now."

"Show me how you kiss," she shrugged. I remember thinking that I kiss my Mum, my Nan, and yes, even my sister as a thank you for presents, so I leaned over and pecked her on the lips. "That's not how you kiss," she said.

"What do you mean?" I asked.

"You open your mouth and put your tongue inside the other person," she explained.

"Really? That sounds horrible."

"No… it's really nice," she told me.

"Who have you done it with then?" I demanded as I couldn't remember her having a steady boyfriend.

"Promise not to tell?"

"Scout's honour," I replied, wanting to know the secret.

"You're not a scout anymore!" she chided me before telling me, "I do it with Rachel."

"Wow," I said, thinking about seeing the two of them kissing.

"It's only until we get boyfriends," she went on to explain. "After all, we don't want to look silly when we do get a boyfriend, so we are practicing with each other."

"That's so neat," I said.

"Do you want to learn so that you know how to do it properly?"

"Sure!"

told me to rub my hand up and down which I did until my arm got tired and I wanted to stop.

That was when she touched me. She rubbed my willy a few times before taking hold of my still immature testicles. I nearly cried out when she gave them a squeeze which was too hard and suddenly the game was over. I put my underpants back on and got into my sleeping back so that she couldn't squeeze me again. I guess that she must have realised that she had hurt me as she got dressed and into her sleeping bag before she gave me more than my fair share of the snacks. The conversation changed to music and we battled against our tiredness until we fell asleep.

It was a couple of weeks later that the second and final time that I played around with my sister happened. It was a week day, still during the summer holidays, and as such my parents were at work. With my sister being fourteen, my parents trusted that she would be responsible enough to not have to have a babysitter, although in those days, we were generally allowed to be adult free during the day anyway.

I was in my room when my sister came in and asked if I wanted to play princes and princesses. I must not have answered in the negative because before I knew it, we were on my bed with me lying on top of her. I wanted to show her that I now knew how to kiss properly, as I'd been practicing on my pillow at night, and my mouth met hers. We traded tongues, her hand gripping the back of my head, forcing me not to break the kiss and it got quite heated. We finally broke the kiss and without a word said, stripped out of our clothes. Again, I lay on top of her and kissed her. Our hands roamed and it was all going very sexy until she pushed me off of her and guided my head lower on her body. She told me to kiss her down there and not knowing it was wrong to do that to your sister, I did. She held my head there for a few minutes before she let me get back up. I asked her to make me feel good and she took hold of my stiffness, giving it a couple of rubs.

However, just like before, when she took hold of my testicles, she gripped them too hard and I squealed out in pain. The moment was over and she left me on my bed, alone, nursing my bruised balls.

If I remember correctly, she got a boyfriend not long after we started back to school, and we never did anything together again, sexually wise. That was fine with me as I hadn't really enjoyed some of it, while I had really enjoyed others, such as the kissing.

Looking back with adult eyes, ignoring the taboo of incest, I don't think that she did anything wrong as such. You hear about brothers who explore with each other and, lacking that brotherly sibling, my sister was there instead. There is also a term called "age appropriateness" which explains about children who explore their burgeoning sexuality and sexual awareness. Being a couple of years either way of each other's age is generally accepted as being normal as long as there was no forceful or threatening behaviour. I look at the experience with my sister as a learning curve of how to kiss, how to touch and how not to be touched. I doubt that my sister even remembers this as it happened some three decades ago, but it stuck in my mind because of so many 'firsts' that I experienced.

It was from there though that I decided that I needed to try to be straight. Or rather than I needed to at least cover my tracks about fancying men and boys by going out with girls again. After all, if I could fake getting excited with my sister, then girls who didn't know me as well would be no problem in fooling. All I needed to do now was figure out which girl to ask out... but that could wait until we were back at school.

The summer holiday continued with football and the like until the inevitable day where my parents took me to the uniform shop to buy my new school uniform. It looked disgusting. It was a medium dark brown blazer, the same

coloured trousers and a brown tie that had thin, diagonal yellow stripes. The PE kit was no better. It was a bright yellow rugby shirt which you could turn inside out and wear as an away strip of brown with a yellow hoop.

And so the first day came around too quickly and, as my Nan lived just down the road from the school, I rode my Raleigh Racer and parked it up at hers before walking up to the school. As we were first years, (we didn't use the school year identities that are around today), we all had to meet up in the main assembly hall where the headmaster welcomed us to the school. He said a lot of largely forgettable things before our names were called out as we were split into our form classes. If you are American, think Home Rooms. Our form classes were where we would go first thing in the morning to have the register taken before going about our daily classes. We'd also meet there after lunch and also had three private study periods each week where we would do homework, allegedly, and our form teacher would make sure that everything was okay with us.

The school year set of pupils were also split into two. Each form class represented one house, I was placed into the red house, Tedder, named after the former Marshall of the Royal Air Force, Arthur Tedder, and we would be combined with the yellows of Cunningham house while the blues and greens of Montgomery and Churchill would make up the other half. I was pleased when I heard Dave called into Churchill as it meant that I would rarely see him but when Paul was also placed into Churchill, my heart sank a little.

As we filed out behind Mrs Smith, our form tutor, I studied my new form mates and was pleased that I recognised a couple of lads from my Primary school but as we walked into our form room, I quickly found that they had already arranged to sit together and I was left looking around the classroom. Unlike the Primary school where we had tables pushed together to make six or eight places,

the tables at the High School were two seater affairs. I looked at the seats available and saw two next to two girls that I didn't know and one next to a boy, also unknown. Taking the safe option, I chose the seat next to the boy.

It's funny how fate works. Had I taken a different seat, my life may have been completely different and I wouldn't be here, writing these words, experiencing all of these feelings and emotions.

Chapter Five – Tuesday 8th September

So the buzzer to my apartment went, making me jump as it always does despite the fact that I knew she was coming round. After all, we had arranged it at the weekend and now, seven thirty on a Tuesday evening, I was about to open up a very personal conversation with a woman who I'd only met half a dozen times before. Yes, I had now known her for several months but we only really saw each other at the writers' group meetings. We were arranging a social group but that hadn't started yet, and with Tony hundreds of miles away in Glasgow, I suddenly felt the need to talk to someone in person who had gone through something similar.

The excuse for her coming round was actually a very valid one. We had read the first chapter of her book a couple of meetings before and I had made a lot of notes on my copy which I had given back to her. Tonight was primarily to go through the notes that I had written, but I knew that we would talk about what had happened to each of us.

I put down my photo album that I had been looking through, finding pictures of myself when I was at that age, and invited her in. She had come armed with a bottle of Mount Gay rum and we finally sat down to talk. It had been a long time coming, as we had initially discussed it in July and now here we were in September and, after a couple of mouthfuls of rum, we got talking.

Talking about what happened to each of us.

Obviously we made a pact that nothing that was said would be repeated to anyone else and that, I think, allowed me a little bit more courage to discuss things with her that I probably wouldn't have. I went into some of the details of timings and who had actually been involved, without naming names, while not actually going into explicit detail. Again, as I mentioned in chapter three, there is a fine line between what I want to say, what I want to write and what I think is acceptable for the readers to read. I have actually now downloaded three or four books by other men and women who were abused as children so that I can get a feel as to what they went through and how they have written.

The first one, which I started yesterday, is called "Starstruck" by Joey Alvarez. It looks an interesting format as he has admitted up front that he isn't a writer and has simply used the transcripts from his therapy sessions as his manuscript.

However, I digress. My friend and I talked for around an hour about it before we got down to going through the notes of her chapter. I had already got my laptop turned on so we also went through some parts of chapter two of my story and she repeated her assertion that she wants to read this. I also showed her some of the photos and she reiterated her feelings of contempt about how men could take a cute boy like I had been and did the things that they did. She also really liked the idea for the title, which is what my story is called, and the idea for the cover.

After she went, I took some photos of the school photograph that was taken in my first year at High School. I emailed it through to the lady who has designed the covers for four of my other books and asked the question about using it but blurring out my face. I'd love for people to see how cute I actually was back in the day, but as I am writing this under a penname and the fact that my parents

will NEVER find out about this, obviously I need to protect my identity.

With a promise to myself to try to call the helpline again on Saturday morning, I think that I am just about ready to tell what happened to me. What happened after that fateful moment of sitting on an empty seat next to a boy that I didn't know. A boy who's impact on my life is the largest influence of how I've turned out, other than being born.

Andrew Michelson

Chapter Six – A New School and a New Friend

I pulled the seat from beneath the table and sat down. I looked at the boy who returned my gaze with a faint smile of hope on his face. He had unruly black hair, a long, thin face and brown eyes. He was slim, not quite as slim as I was, but still had a bit of baby fat on him I guess. Not really knowing what else to do, I sat down next to him and said "Hi."

"Hello. I'm Andy," he said.

"Me too! Well, Andrew actually," I replied, cringing at myself as I caught myself correcting my name. So much for being cool.

We got talking about what schools we had come from and I found out that he lived in one of the small villages a few miles out of town. I felt bad for him when he told me that it was just him and his Dad as his Mum had died when he was very young but he explained that his Dad was great and his Uncle was always coming around as well.

This got my back up slightly as I realised that he must be all boy, brought up by two men, so I knew that I had to act like a normal boy, like one who fancies girls. To be honest, it wouldn't be a problem around him as, while he wasn't ugly, he wasn't the best looking boy either. So I didn't really fancy him as such.

However, now thrust into a much larger school, one that had around three hundred pupils per school grade and

there were three grades. This meant that there were some four hundred and fifty boys attending the school. Of course, out of those four hundred and fifty, I found a lot of them attractive and I alternated from wanting to be friends with them and hang around with them to not wanting to be anywhere near them in case my secret got out. Being gay at this school was certainly not something that you wanted exposed as the bullies made their presence known.

My first experience with a bully was within the first few weeks of the year. A group of us first years were playing outside on the field at lunchtime when several of the year two boys started picking on us. It was the usual pushing us around and tripping us over but, to my and the bullies surprise, a lad from year three came over and stopped them. He was being backed up by several of his mates and I recognised him from a couple of years previous as he had gone to the same Primary School as me. Dean came from a large family, all of them known as tough nuts and here he was, telling the year two lads to shove off and leave me alone. While I thought that it was great that he'd come in to save me and my friends, I did discover an ulterior motive in that he fancied my sister, despite her being a year older than him and no longer at the High school. From then on, the year two lads left us alone.

However, it did reinforce my opinion that being different wasn't something that I needed to be, so I tried my best to fit in to the norm. I did ask a couple of girls out, but I had obviously set my sights too high as I was rebuffed with giggles and laughter echoing in my ears. So I became just one of the lads, one of the pack who kept themselves to themselves in their small groups.

I enjoyed all of my lessons, with the exception of French which was very difficult, but I soon found one of my previous favourite subjects was now well down my list, Physical Education.

PE was now a major source of embarrassment for me. At Primary School, changing for PE mainly meant taking off your trousers and shirt and putting on your shorts and top. At the High School, showers were compulsory to the point where one of the teachers would stand and make sure that we all took one. The shower block was basically part of the changing rooms itself, being a painted brick wall with openings at either end. The shower heads were lined up on the two walls and we basically had to strip naked, walk with our towels to one of the two ends and hang up said towel. Then we'd step inside and wash before coming back out, dripping wet and getting our towel to dry off before getting dressed. This totally exposed your body to your peers for at least a couple of minutes. I sometimes wonder with adult eyes and experiences if any of the teachers were perverts, watching us naked boys, but as far as I am aware, none of them ever did anything other than watch us.

The showers were a double edged sword for me. On the plus side, it allowed me to sneak looks at the boys that I fancied, seeing them naked and filling my mind with images that would keep me occupied at night. The down side was that it reinforced my lack of self-confidence about my own body, with a lot of the boys having bigger penises than me. I should have realised that, being born at the end of February, most of the boys were older than me so the chances were that they would be more developed. Six months is a long time when you are only eleven after all, but still, my lack of confidence about my bits was certainly taking more and more hits as the larger boys had no problem in parading themselves around the changing rooms.

My friendship with my desk mate, Andy, was slowly building but took a step up on one of the private study periods that we had. I like to think that I'm fairly smart, having tested as an adult with an I.Q. of one hundred and thirty six and at school, I was in either set one or set two

for all of my subjects. Andy, however, wasn't the brightest spark and was not higher than a set three and mostly was in sets four or five out of five. So it was with a bit of self-confidence and, maybe a little ego boosting, that I started to help him with his school work. I was, and am, a whizz at maths, and happily spent time showing him how to solve algebra problems as well as trigonometry, and also helped out with the sciences.

Of course, being in different sets for all of our subjects except for P.E. meant that we only saw each other at form times and at breaks. We each developed our own groups of friends, while still trying to share those groups with each other.

I found out that he'd made friends with a lad called Phil, who I recognised as being in some of my classes at infant school and primary school. While I hadn't been good friends with him, we did get along and, with Andy now a firm friend of his, the three of us would spend time together. Phil lived in the same town as me, and we started to go around to his house at weekends to hang out. Andy would have to be dropped off by his Dad or Uncle, who would then pick him up as well. I found myself in the awkward situation of almost being a third wheel as they were both very much into horror comics, while I didn't like them at all. However, the fact that I needed Andy's friendship at school kept me quietly reading the comics but I also found myself getting attracted to Phil.

Phil was a small boy, with dark brown hair, slim body and a funny sense of humour. I remember fantasising that maybe, just maybe, I'd walk into the lounge if we were watching television or his bedroom and find the two of them making out. Then perhaps, I could join in. Of course, it didn't happen but we did get close.

Phil knew the man who ran the local video store and so, despite only being eleven, he could get his hands on eighteen rated movies. They were called X-rated in those days. However, his tastes in movies, like his comics, were

of the horror genre and I can clearly remember getting scared nearly to death by watching 'An American Werewolf in London' years before I should have been watching it. The pair of them made some comment about Jenny Aguter's body before Phil stepped it up a level with the film the following week. 'The Exorcist' is still considered by many to be one of the greatest horror movies of all time, I think to do with the fact that there is no backing music throughout. While they watched it for the horror aspect, Andy took great delight in the part of the film where Linda Blair uses a crucifix in a way that it really shouldn't have been used. That section of the film was rewound and played again several times and I couldn't help but notice that my friends were rubbing their crotches while they watched. Not wanting to be seen as being weird or anything, I openly rubbed my own, pretending to be interested with the movie on screen but more interested in watching my friends out of the corner of my eyes.

It wasn't long after that incident that my own sexual experimentations altered forever. At least on how I masturbated. As I mentioned before, my favourite position was to have a pillow rolled up under my groin and I would hump into it. This caused friction on my penis and it would bring me to my climax before I unrolled it, put it back under my head and went to sleep. That was all well and good while I was still prepubescent and having dry orgasms. The first time that I squirted, I literally thought I'd peed myself and my pillow. I was distraught, having thought that I'd gotten over wetting the bed, but when I looked, I saw that it wasn't pee after all. It was a slimy fluid that smelled funny. I dried it off with my underwear and went to sleep wondering what the hell it was.

I didn't know who to ask, so I kept quiet about it. Had I broken something? Why was it always me that stuff was happening to and not to other boys? If only my Dad had taken the time and had the guts to have the birds and the

bees talk with me, I wouldn't have had to go through weeks of torturous worry.

It was in the term leading up to Christmas break that I finally discovered what was happening to me. On one of the private study periods, all of the boys from my half of the school year were told to report to the lecture theatre. None of us knew what for... what had we done wrong? Who was in trouble? It turned out nobody was... or was it all of us?

We took our seats and in walked the two male PE teachers. I've no idea why it was the PE teachers and not science but I've found out from other friends later in life that they had similar experiences. They told us to quiet down and started explaining that, for the next three weeks, we would be getting lessons about our bodies and how they worked. I was already doing biology so didn't understand why the PE teachers would be taking these lessons until they started explaining about our boy bits. This was it! This was the sex education that we'd all been looking forward to!

Of course, most of us got very embarrassed at the diagrams and pictures that were put up showing the penises of various men and boys, and most of us felt a bit sick when the pictures of women's vaginas came on screen. They explained how men and women made babies and I learned what it was that was literally coming out of the end of my own penis. It all made sense to me now and I restarted my masturbation at night at a frantic pace, to make up for the lost time where I had stopped. However, I did swap my pillow for a hot water bottle, sneakily filling it with warm water before humping that. I found that if I positioned it just right, the hard part of it where you filled it up would press into my now growing testicles and make me feel even better when I shot. With the bottle being warm, any ejaculate would dry overnight, hiding the evidence of what I was doing. The bottle must have

smelled something awful, unless my Mum washed it and if she did, it meant she must have known what I was doing.

Just before Christmas, Phil dropped the bombshell on us that his Mum was moving down south to go and live with her parents. Phil's Dad wasn't in the picture; he hadn't died, just left them years before, and so they had always been struggling money wise.

This left Andy and myself relying more and more on each other as we became best friends. Of course, with Andy living out of the town, it cut down the time we could spend after school, so we soon got in a routine of either Andy walking home with me and his Dad picking him up after a couple of hours, or I would get on the school bus that dropped us off in his village and his Dad would bring me home.

We would hang out, playing on his games console and I'd also help with his homework, something that got me praise from his Dad. While the praise probably massaged my ego, it also started to massage strange feelings that were growing inside me. His Dad was, in my memory, a hunk. He was tall and muscular, with dark hair and dark eyes and I found myself wanting him to be pleased with whatever I did. I thought nothing about helping Andy with chores around his house, something that I had to be bribed with pocket money at my own house, and my reward from his Dad was a pat on the shoulder, or the arm, or even better, a brief one armed hug. I found that my night time fantasies soon started to change from being with the boys from my school to the hunk that was Andy's Dad. I relished being hugged by him as my own Dad wasn't particular hands on so I lapped up the physical contact that he gave me and it carried over into my solo pleasures at night.

Christmas that year was the year that I discovered Santa didn't really exist. Now, being eleven I had an inkling that there wasn't something really truthful about a fat bloke

who could visit all of the children in the whole world in one evening and deliver all of those presents. After all, where would he put them? His sack wasn't that big, was it? And flying reindeer? But, like all parents with their children, mine had done a good job in lying to me, sorry… convincing me that he was real. The sherry and mince pie was always drunk and eaten and, up to that point, my sister and I still woke up around two AM to creep downstairs to see the amount of presents underneath the tree. We knew every creaky floorboard. I found out afterwards that my sister knew but played along at my parents request to keep the magic alive for me.

A Christmas Eve tradition for my family was that we went and visited our relatives in their respective villages. My Dad was the youngest of five, and my Aunts and Uncles were no slouches when it came to popping out cousins either. Most of my cousins were a lot older than me, some by thirty years or so, but we were still a fairly close family. I seem to recall that we had a period of about five years where we had around three or four weddings per year of my second cousins but I digress.

This particular Christmas Eve evening, we were coming out of one of my Aunt and Uncle's house, walking unsteadily back to the car having had more than my fair share of sherry, when my sister slipped on a section of black ice and went flying. She immediately started crying, which I knew meant that she had really hurt herself as she didn't normally cry at anything, and when my Dad helped her to her feet, she couldn't put any weight on her ankle. So we ended up in A&E at the city's main hospital. It took forever for her to be seen and I was panicking because I hadn't hung up my stocking. What if Santa had been to visit our house before we got home and I missed out on the little treats and chocolates that I always got?

We got home at around three in the morning and I rushed inside, ignoring the hobbling sibling by my side… it turned out that it was just a sprain, but to my horror, there

were no presents underneath the Christmas tree. The time was well after my sister and I normally woke up to creep downstairs so it just didn't fathom why he hadn't called. Thoughts ran through my head about how naughty I'd been all year before my Dad told me to go to bed and he mentioned to my Mum about getting the presents out of the cupboards. So… thank you very much to my sister for ruining the Christmas magic for me!

That Christmas was special though in a couple of ways. Firstly, I received my very own pool cue. It was a beauty. It was a three piece cue which unscrewed in the middle and had a small six inch section at the base. That piece was weighted so that you could have a light or heavy cue depending on how you played. I will talk more about my cue in later chapters.

The second event was my first ever viewing of a porno. With school closed for around two to three weeks, Andy and I had to beg our respective parents to drop each other off so that we could hang out together. It was in between Christmas Day and New Year's Eve that I had gone over to Andy's and we were got a bit bored after playing his latest games on his console. He asked if I wanted to watch something naughty on their video recorder. Of course, Christmas had now passed and, with the knowledge that there was no Santa Claus, I didn't see the need to be on my best behaviour any more. I can't remember where his Dad was, I'm sure he was around somewhere, but it was just the two of us in the lounge. He flicked on the television and put a tape into the machine and pressed play. I've no recollection of what the title was, what the plot was… if there even was one, but on screen were a collection of men and women having sex. Proper sex. They were completely naked and you could see everything. I know that I got an erection and glanced at Andy in embarrassment but he was openly rubbing the front of his jeans. Taking that as an okay to do the same, I did as well. I kept stopping when I felt myself getting too close,

because I didn't want to make a mess in my jeans, but Andy just kept going until he let out a loud moan. I couldn't believe that my best mate had just rubbed himself to a finish but made no indication that he had to clean up, the reason for which I was to find out the following weekend.

Having agreed that it was really neat, we went back to his room before his Dad found us watching his videos as Andy put it, and I thought that we were so sneaky. We had a sleepover that night, sharing Andy's large bed as we did sometimes, and he rabbited on about the video, especially the size of the women's boobs. Of course, I had been more interested in looking at the men, but I tried to play along, keeping up my straight act. I was painfully stiff but pretended to be tired and rolled on my side facing away from him to 'go to sleep'. I soon felt the bed moving slightly and realised that Andy was playing with himself but I fought off the desire to turn over and watch him.

The next few days, I couldn't keep the made up image in my mind of my best mate doing it and so, when he came over for a sleepover at mine a few days later, I knew that I had to do something otherwise I would go crazy. But what? How could I approach this straight lad and ask if he wanted to play around with me? For the first couple of hours, we just hung around as normal, watching television or reading my comics, until my parents decided that they were going down to the working mens club for a couple of hours. Did we want to go with them? I immediately piped up that we were okay staying on our own, my sister having been dropped off at a friend's house, and with warnings not to break anything, we were left alone. My mind was going ten to the dozen as I finally had Andy on his own but how could I instigate it? I remember glancing over at a photo frame that had a montage of photos of me and I saw a picture from a couple of years before that was of Paul, Dave and myself.

The rape game! Would he be up for it? My sister had a collection of wigs for dressing up from when she was younger and I told Andy to stay where he was in the lounge while I went and got a couple of things. I ran upstairs, into the sacred, out of bounds territory of my sister's bedroom and quickly found one of the wigs at the bottom of a cupboard. I grabbed one of my teddies from my room... yes I did still have a collection of them at eleven years old, and headed back down.

I explained the game to Andy, emphasising that it was about a man feeling up a woman to cover my ulterior motives, and popped a stiffy when he agreed without hesitation. Not wanting to be seen as being too eager to feel him up, I volunteered to go first as the woman. I put on the wig, much to his hilarity, and pushed the teddy up my jumper. I let him grab me, but unlike in Paul's room where we had a bed to fall onto, I hadn't had enough foresight about that. I let him push me up against one of the walls and he grabbed hold of the teddy, groping my boobies. I remember feeling his breath on the back of my neck but before anything happened, he let me go.

He said that it was a good game and he would now be the woman so I could take my turn. We repeated the actions, with me pushing him against the wall and I couldn't help but do what Dave did to me and I pushed my groin into Andy's backside. I guess that he must have felt it because he suggested that we pulled the cushions from the sofa and spread them onto the floor so that next time, the man could lie on top of the woman. That seemed like a good idea and we made quick work of making a pile on the floor.

I put the teddy up my jumper once again but Andy told me that I didn't need to wear the wig as it had made his head itch. I was happy enough not to wear it so we set it up, with me walking past him. He grabbed me and we "fell" over onto the pile of cushions. As he groped my boobies, this time he followed my actions and started to

hump himself into my backside. I could feel him through both of our jeans and I knew that he was bigger than me, which put a slight downer on it, but that was soon forgotten as his body weight was pushing me into the cushions. This had the effect of causing friction through my jeans and I soon found myself past the point of worrying about any potential mess. I remember the feeling of dampness in my underwear and my body shuddering underneath his and I laid there until I felt and heard Andy in the throes of his own orgasm. I now knew what the word was, having gone through sex ed! As he rolled off me, he had a big grin on his face, one which I am sure was replicated on mine. I remember the next part of the conversation very well!

"That was great," Andy said. "Come on, it's your turn."

"No, it's okay," I replied. "Let's go and get cleaned up." I was referring to the sticky mess that I was sure would be in both of our underwear.

"Okay, I guess your parents wouldn't like us making the mess on the floor," he sighed.

"No, I meant to clean up our cum," I explained.

"Huh?"

"You know, our seeds," I'd giggled. "I am all sticky and it's soaking through my pants." I pointed to the faint, but steadily growing wet spot in my jeans.

"You can shoot?" he gasped. "No way!"

"Way!" I replied. "Can't you?" Andy was about four months older than me so I was surprised. I guess that I must have been an early developer in that sense… just a shame that my penis didn't keep up.

"I don't believe you," he shot back. "Show me."

I pointed again to the crotch of my jeans but it wasn't enough proof for him so I undid the button and zip of my jeans and pulled them and my pants down far enough to show the mess, but still covering up my now shrinking penis. He shocked me by feeling my mess, rubbing it on

me and his fingers, sniffing it as if to make sure that it wasn't pee.

"Wow!" he said.

Despite my desire to get naked with him, I left him in the lounge and went upstairs and wiped myself down with a flannel. When I came back downstairs, he'd put the cushions back on the sofa. He didn't mention anything again, so I didn't... at least until bedtime.

My bed was just a single so we didn't share it like we did at his house. My Mum had a foam mattress topper that she used when she went camping with the Guides and I would sleep on that on the floor while giving up my bed to my friend. As we got changed for bed, I watched Andy out of the corner of my eye as he stripped down to his underpants and I did the same. I climbed under the duvet and we started talking again about things that boys our age talked about. Finally, the topic changed to what had happened earlier.

"I still can't believe you can shoot," he'd said. "I mean, no offence, but you're still so small. I can't shoot yet."

"It's really neat," I giggled. "But it's very messy. I wish that I couldn't shoot."

"But it means you're getting to be a man," he moaned. "Come on, show me again."

Looking back, why I didn't throw caution to the wind and pull my duvet back and get naked, I don't know. However, I simply grabbed the nearest thing that I could use to catch my ejaculate, which happened to be a piece of paper, rolled up my pillow and humped away until I came. I shot onto the paper and handed it over to him. We must have been making too much noise as my sister came into my room and demanded that we gave her some of the snacks that we were obviously fighting over. Fortunately Andy was a quick thinker and chucked her a couple of chocolate bars and she left us to it. I never did find that bit of paper the next day.

That weekend took our play dates, as such, in a whole different direction. We only played on the consoles or watched television when we felt that we needed to make an appearance in front of our parents. Secretly we were in whosever's bedroom, humping away on top of each other until we got our feelings. Andy suggested that I used one of his socks the first time and I slipped it into my underpants and covered up my willy with it. He said that he did his own laundry so his Dad wouldn't find out, which put my mind at rest.

After the first couple of times, Andy suggested that we strip to just our underwear and then suggested that instead of him laying on my back, that I should lie face up and he would hump against my groin. I'd agreed, wanting to feel him against me but again, it was Andy who took things up a step. As he laid on top of me, humping away, his face was hovering just above mine and with no question asked, he kissed me on the lips. I tried to pull away at first but he was slightly heavier than me and he held me there. I gave in to my feelings, not that I really fought them, and kissed him back just as my sister had taught me. It was amazing, kissing someone who wasn't related to you and we were both nearly naked as well. As we finished, he looked at me with a question in his eyes.

"It's just like we're practicing, isn't it?" I suggested, not wanting him to think that I really wanted more.

"Yeah... that's right. I think we need to practice, don't we?"

He leaned forward and kissed me again. I don't know how long we kissed for but when I heard his Dad coming up the stairs, I pushed him off me and we started playing one of the games that we had already set up. His Dad came into the room and I blushed as I realised that I was sat in just my underwear that had a big wet patch in the front. He stood there, asking us about our day, what we wanted for dinner and generally seemed to be in hurry to leave the room. Normally I wouldn't have minded, being

that I had a crush on him, but to be sat there virtually naked was really embarrassing.

Nothing was said to me while I was there about it. In fact, Andy had even suggested staying in our underwear but there was no way that I could do that. I put my jeans back on for dinner but I did stay shirtless. The three of us watched a video that evening, I can't remember what it was but Andy's Dad was sat in the middle of the two of us and had his arms around our shoulders. It felt really nice, having him hug me to him and I remember falling asleep onto him. When I woke up, I was in Andy's bed and found that I was in my other pair of underpants. Andy told me that his Dad had suggested that I shouldn't sleep in my soiled ones and they had removed them. The thought that his Dad had seen me naked caused me to really start fantasising about him, but of course, he was a man, and men didn't fancy boys… did they?

Andrew Michelson

Chapter Seven – Wednesday 23rd September

Well, Tuesday evening didn't work out as planned. I knew that it was the big Birmingham derby match in the cup on television and I definitely wanted to be in my local to watch it. While I don't support either Aston Villa or Birmingham, there were enough people that I knew did and I wanted to enjoy the match with them. So I rushed home from work, had a snack and by six fifteen, I was counting down the minutes to six thirty, which was when the helpline was manned by the male volunteer.

I picked up my phone and nervously rang the number. I had already had the opening conversation about a hundred times in my head. What should I say? How should I say it? What did I actually want to gain from ringing them? How much detail should I go into? It's a bit like writing this journal.

However, it seemed like the volunteer must be either a Villa fan or a Blues fan because for some strange reason, he wasn't going to be there tonight. Did I want to talk to a lady? Knowing about how personal this was going to be, I just didn't feel right talking to her. My fellow writer one thing, which I didn't get to the nitty gritty, but to describe exactly what had happened to me with an anonymous woman was entirely different.

So I said thanks but no thanks and told her I would ring on Saturday when he was back on the helpline.

Now faced with an hour to kill before going to the pub, I decided to re-read the previous chapter. Is it wrong that as I read my experiences with Andy, I sort of enjoyed the memories of my experimentations with him? I can clearly remember that first time that we played the rape game, and making a mess in my underpants. I can clearly remember that first kiss with Andy, even though I didn't fancy him, he was still the first boy or man that I kissed like that. Those were good, fun times that I liked to remember. Those were the "normal, coming of age" experiments that I have read about. Those were the experiences that have led me to wear a lot of rose tinted glasses when I've looked back at my memories in previous times.

Ever since talking with my author friend, I have reluctantly taken off those glasses to have a long, hard look at what happened to me all of those years before. The remaining chapters will be difficult to read, I am sure, but please remember, it will probably be more difficult for me to write these chapters as I will be tearing down some of the barriers that I had installed in my mind.

I am going to write these chapters as I remember them happening. I will probably alternate my language a lot during it from what I used to call things back then to the adult names of things when it gets uncomfortable.

None of the following is supposed to be titillating in any way but it will go into some detail about the sexual activity. Some of my memories are crystal clear, about conversations and events, while others are fuzzy, either faded by time or blocked by my own mind to protect myself. While I will remember parts in detail and parts not fully, I will try to write them as I remember them happening. You must take into account when you read it that my original, rose tinted memories were of enjoyment for the most part but as I have been revisiting it, I am realising about how much of what I believed was what I

was made to believe. I hope that this comes across from my "looking at it with adult eyes" comments.

This is my story about how my sexual experimentation with Andy was moved to another level, and then some. This is how my now adult sexual life was defined.

Andrew Michelson

Chapter Eight - Escalation

I couldn't wait for the next sleepover at Andy's. My parents were beginning to complain about how many sleepovers we were having, which I now realise was more to do with lack of money and it being another mouth to feed for a few days each month, when Andy's Dad said that he didn't mind if we stopped alternating and had the majority at their house. When my parents started to counter argue, he simply said that there weren't many boys of Andy's age in the village and it was nice for him to have someone to hang out with. We both pleaded with my parents to let us continue and it was finally agreed that, unless something came up, I would now go home with Andy on the bus every Friday afternoon, stay over and come back on the Saturday. Matt, Andy's Dad, said that he would bring me home so that they didn't need to worry about coming over.

Both Andy and I were delighted as it gave us more privacy at his house than at mine, what with my sister who had an annoying habit of not knocking on my closed bedroom door when she wanted to come in. That week at school seemed to take forever. How Andy and I avoided a) getting into trouble and a detention or b) outing ourselves to the school, I have no idea. We kept giving each other knowing looks about what we were going to get up to on Friday evening and I was in a constant state of arousal. So much so that I even seemed to lose interest in

some of my boy crushes. After all, what use was a fantasy when I had a willing partner?

Friday came around and we found ourselves on the school bus. Obviously we were not on the back seats as that was strictly the territory of the Grammar School boys who shared the bus with the High School. We kept ourselves away from them, sitting in the middle of the bus and we were rubbing our legs against each other. I had to put my bag in front of me when we got up to get off the bus as I had grown excited about what we were going to get up to.

When we got into his house, his Dad was still at work. I guess in those days, it was slightly less frowned upon to leave boys of our age on our own without adult supervision. We certainly weren't complaining! We dumped our school bags in the hallway as normal and went up to his room. We wasted no time in stripping down to our underpants and stood there looking at each other for a moment before giggling like the naughty schoolboys that I guess we were. Andy made the first move and stepped over to me and wrapped his arms around me. He kissed me and I responded. He moved me backwards until we toppled onto his bed, with him on top of me as normal. He started to grind himself into me but this time, before I made a mess in my underwear I managed to stop him. I still remember the way that the conversation went.

"Why did you stop me? I was just getting close," he complained.

"Me too, that's why," I replied.

"But why?"

"I don't want to make a mess again. Can I use one of your socks again, like before?"

He picked up one of the socks he'd been wearing all day at school and sniffed it. He grinned as he covered my nose with it.

"Get it off me!" I screamed as I nearly gagged on the smell of sweaty feet.

"I've got an idea," he said, throwing the sock on the floor. "Why don't we, like, just take off our pants?"

"What? And do it naked?"

"Yeah… it'll be neat."

I didn't really need to argue as I now had the chance to actually touch another boy who would be naked. I had seen Andy naked before but only in the changing rooms and he was never in a state of arousal. I knew that he was bigger than me but I didn't realise just how developed he was. We both stood up and neither of us seemed to want to go first in getting naked. So Andy said we'd do it together on the count of three and when he hit that magic number, we both pulled down our underwear. I fought the desire to cover myself and took a long look at my now naked friend.

He was erect, obviously as he'd been humping against me moments earlier and he was big. Well, bigger than me easily anyway. I remember commenting about it and he got a ruler to measure us both. I measured in at a measly touch over three inches long while he topped the five inch mark. He said that maybe he could make mine longer, which I just looked at him questioningly, and he reached out and took hold of my penis. He gave it a few tugs and I felt like I'd gone to heaven. Someone else was wanking me and it felt wonderful. I was nervous as he touched my testicles, remembering the pain of my sister's grip but he was gentle. I reached down and took hold of his, feeling another penis for the first time in my life. I tried to do what he was doing but must not have been doing it quite right as he said to get back onto the bed. I climbed on and he got on top of me in the usual position for humping. He lay fully on top of me, trapping our penises between us and started humping. He kissed me again and before I knew it, I was frantically pushing myself against him until I shot. Andy soon finished his own orgasm and got a

flannel from the bathroom to clean me up. We put our underpants back on and I was going to put on my jeans but he persuaded me that I didn't need to, so I just followed him back downstairs, dressed only in underpants.

We were watching television when his Dad came home and I watched a little envious as Andy got a big hug from his Dad. My Dad wasn't a hugger. Matt must have seen my expression as he told me to get up and give him a hug as well. I wasn't going to turn down the chance to hug my crush but I was surprised when Matt's hands travelled down my back and onto my cotton covered bottom. He held me close for a few moments and I felt myself get hard before he released me. My face must have been bright red as he chuckled and ruffled my hair, telling me that it was natural for a boy of my age to 'throw wood'.

We went back to watching television, had dinner at the table still dressed in just our underwear before Matt went to get changed. When he came back downstairs, he was only in his underwear. I sort of sniggered as they were y-fronts and got immediately tickle attacked. Now, I was, and I guess still am, very ticklish in my armpits and on the soles of my feet and the pair of them took full advantage. Of course, I was very erect throughout but with his words ringing in my ears, I tried not to get embarrassed. Andy also seemed to be hard while there was an impressive bulge in the front of Matt's y-fronts.

They finally let me up and we sat on the couch to watch television. Like before, Matt sat in the middle with his arms draped over both of our shoulders. I snuggled into him, loving the warmth from his chest against my own, small frame. I tried to stay awake but they must have tired me out with the tickling because I woke up as Matt was carrying me up to Andy's room. It felt nice, being in his strong arms so I pretended to go back to sleep while he carried me. He put me in Andy's bed and I remember him stroking my hair before he kissed my forehead. He told Andy not to wake me, to let me sleep but that he wanted

to talk to him. They went into Matt's room and I couldn't help but have to get myself off. I found Andy's smelly sock and used it to catch my mess before falling asleep, so I don't know how long they talked for but Andy was in bed when I woke the following morning.

We humped each other again before we got up for breakfast and I helped him with his homework before Matt told us that it was time for me to go home. He drove both of us to my house where they came in for a drink, my Dad giving Matt one of his tins of John Smith's while Andy and I had milk. And then they were off and it would be two days before I saw my best mate again.

What we did that Friday night was repeated for about a month as I grew into liking the feel of Andy's body on top of me. I lost my self-consciousness about being nearly naked in front of Matt, quite happily being in just my underpants, even to the extent that when Andy's Uncle Gerry came around on one of the Saturday mornings, I didn't bat an eyelid either. I loved the hugs that were now the regular greeting between Matt and myself and, at nights during the week, I would hug one of my pillows pretending it was him. I even started to kiss the pillow. Weird? I guess I was.

It was getting close to my twelfth birthday, about a fortnight before, when the next part of my education began. It was one of the weekends where I was spending both Friday and Saturday night and we had done our usual Friday routine. Got off the bus, ran up to Andy's room, stripped completely, kissed and humped each other until we were exhausted and got into our underpants to watch television. Matt had come home but said that he had a report to write so he would be in the dining room and could we not make too much noise. We were not to disturb him and he would be at least a couple of hours.

Andy took this as free ticket to get into his Dad's porn collection and he put on one that had two men and a

woman. Each of the men took it in turns to have sex with her and one even put his willy in the woman's mouth.

"So she's a cocksucker!" I giggled as I massaged my groin through my pants.

"Yeah... wait for this bit, it's really neat," Andy replied.

We watched as the man pulled his penis out of her mouth and ejaculated over her face.

"Fab, eh?" Andy pressed.

I was in awe. It was the first time that I had seen a man actually shoot his stuff. Andy was still having dry orgasms, something that I could at least rib him about when he started on the smallness of my penis. It would be just after his thirteenth birthday before he finally made the white stuff.

"That looks so good," I gasped out. "I wonder what it's like?"

"What?"

"Sucking a dick... I mean, having your dick sucked," I stammered, trying to cover my mistake.

"Do you want to try?"

I looked at him and saw that he wasn't taking the mickey, he was serious about it.

"But then you'd be a cocksucker!" The term was very derogatory, even back then. It was the favourite insult doing the rounds at school.

"It would be okay as long as we don't tell no-one," he said. "I mean, I've not told anyone at school about what we do. Have you?"

"Of course not! I don't want people to think that I'm queer," I replied quickly. "I suppose it's a bit like the kissing, isn't it?" I added.

"What is?"

"Well, at some point when we're older, we're gonna get our dicks sucked so it would be good to know how it feels."

That was all Andy needed and he jumped on top of me. He kissed me as he pulled down my pants. He felt me and

as I was already hard from watching the porno, he lowered his head and put his mouth over my penis. I can't put on paper what I felt, that first time, but I know that it was the best thing ever in my life to that moment. I didn't even think about what would happen when I shot but Andy didn't complain. I just laid there, basking in the exaltation that comes with an orgasm when he nudged me.

"Your turn," he said simply.

He was standing in front of me naked, having already shucked his own underwear. Now, I didn't want to be known as a cocksucker, but having just been on the receiving end of my first blowjob, I could always play it off that it was trade. I tried to do what Andy had done to me but, being a virgin at it, I wasn't doing a very good job. Andy must have been getting frustrated because he took hold of my head with his hands, held me still and, without mincing my words, fucked my mouth. I remember coughing and gagging a few times and by the end of it, my eyes had tears in them. It was the first time that Andy had ever been that aggressive with me but somehow it was me who ended up apologising for not being able to suck him correctly. He shrugged, said "no problem" and told me that I would get better the more that we did it.

All thoughts of what that meant were lost as he launched into a wrestling match with me and we were soon rolling around on the carpet, giggling as we fought for control over each other. It was only a cough that alerted us to Matt's presence in the room. He'd come in and was sat on the sofa, watching us wrestle with a glass of coke in his hand, well it actually turned out to be whiskey and coke. He had stripped down to his underwear, like normal. I began to panic on two counts. Firstly, the porno was still playing and I was afraid that we'd be in so much trouble for watching it. I didn't fancy getting smacked on my bare ass, something that Andy had told me his Dad did to him. Secondly, the pair of us were stark bollock naked. I started to scramble in the direction of my underpants when Matt

told me to stop. He said something along the lines that as he'd already seen us, there didn't seem any reason to cover up. He said that a body was a beautiful thing, especially a boy's body and that I had a very beautiful body. It was the first time anyone had called me beautiful.

I watched as Andy sat down next to his Dad and so I did the same. It felt naughty but then again, I wasn't an angel. Matt wrapped his arms around us as always just as there was a loud groan from the television. He made some comment about this being a good video and there it was… I was watching a porno, naked, while my crush had his arm around me. I can't remember much about the video but I do remember trying to hide my erection from Matt, who told me not to. It was a normal reaction to watching a sexy film. I could see that it must be true because I could see that his penis was tenting his y-fronts.

My eyes were further widened before we went bed by Andy openly masturbating while he was sat by the side of his Dad and, as much as I ached to join in, I just couldn't. I asked Andy about it when we went to bed and he said that his Dad was cool and had showed him how to do it and that they were very open about sex talks and stuff. I asked about us staying naked in front of his Dad and he giggled and said that normally, if it is just them in the house, they actually go naked all the time. I remember asking about his Dad's body, how big was his dick, was he hairy and I must have shown a little too much interest in Matt because that is when Andy asked me if I was gay.

I didn't know what to say in reply, fearful that my secret would be the end of our friendship. After all, I'd hidden it from him while we had touched each other, humped and kissed each other and finally sucked each other and I thought he would be mad at me. He said that he thought that he was so it was okay if I was as well. That lifted a huge weight off my shoulders. Finally I had someone that I could talk to about how I fancied boys at school, how I thought about the sex stuff that we did and how I'd like to

do with some of our school peers. Of course, he wanted to know who I fancied and we traded names, giggling like girls as we gave our opinions on each other's choices.

Andy suddenly said that he fancied Gary Shaw, who was a footballer who played for Aston Villa. This was a huge development for me because if he fancied a man, then surely it was okay for me to do so as well. It took some cajoling by him but I finally admitted in a small voice that I had a crush on his Dad. He said that it was cool or something like that and that if I wasn't embarrassed about things, then he would tell his Dad that I was okay to be naked. Then his Dad would also go naked and I could see his dick. That made me super horny and we basically spent the rest of the night trading blowjobs. I think I must have got the hang of it by the third or fourth one as he no longer held my head and let me be in charge.

The following morning, I woke up to Andy playing with me and we humped before getting up to go to the bathroom to wash. It took a lot of courage on my part but I didn't put on my underpants and walked naked to the bathroom. Fortunately, or not, Matt was already downstairs and after washing, I sat waiting for Andy to do the same. He came back in and asked if I was ready to go down for breakfast. I think he saw my nerves so he took my hand and held it as we walked down the stairs and into the kitchen.

I nearly crapped myself as I saw Andy's Uncle Gerry sat at the table with a cuppa but Andy held on to my hand so that I couldn't run back upstairs. Gerry just chuckled and Matt made some comment about what a nice picture to start the morning with. Andy pulled me to the table and we sat down. At least the table covered my embarrassment. Matt asked me if I was okay with being naked and I slowly nodded. Andy said that he'd explained last night about how they normally went without clothes and that I was going to join them. Again, Matt asked if that was correct and that I wouldn't tell anyone. I shook

my head, wanting to see him and not wanting to ruin the chance that I had. Gerry stood up and started taking his shirt off and said that he was glad that I was joining their club, as he called it. I couldn't believe that I was sat in a kitchen watching a grown man strip in front of me.

Gerry wasn't a great looking guy but, like Matt, he must have worked out as his body was in great shape. Of course, my eyes were drawn to his groin as he pulled his underwear down and stepped out of them. His penis looked huge, to me anyway. There was a big, thick bush of hair above it and it was slowly hardening.

I saw Matt begin to take his clothes off as well, now that he had finished cooking breakfast. I probably drooled as his naked form came into view and the thought flashed through my mind about how it would feel to have his penis in my mouth instead of Andy's. I shook that thought away because he was obviously straight, being a Dad.

We spent the rest of the day naked. Their back garden was private with a big wooden, panelled fence around it and no houses over looked it so we played catch outside. It felt so free to be naked outside and it was like a whole new world had opened up around me.

When we got cold, we went inside to watch television and, looking back with my adult eyes, I should have realised that there was something more to them than I had thought. As we sat down, Gerry took the armchair while Matt and I sat on the sofa. Instead of sitting on the spare seat of the sofa, Andy switched the light off and sat on Gerry's lap in the chair. There wasn't a lot of light from the television but I did see Gerry stroking Andy's chest and legs. However, I was sat on the other side of Matt so didn't see properly and with Matt's arm around me, I melted into his side like I normally did. The warmth of his body and the earlier activity must have tired me out as, like had become a habit, I drifted off to sleep next to Matt.

I woke up in Andy's bed during the night and was alone. I needed the bathroom so I went and on the way back I crept to Matt's closed bedroom door. I could hear the sounds similar to those from the porno and both Matt's and Gerry's voices whispering quietly. At the time, still being quite naïve although I was now growing more sexually aware, I didn't really understand what they were talking about. They said something about the boy being "ready to pluck and take the cherry" and that they should let "him" do it first just in case. I heard Andy's voice from inside the room and thought that he must have gone in there to talk to them so I crept away and went back to Andy's room.

With my adult eyes, I obviously now know what was happening in the room and what they were talking about. But at the time, I had full trust in my best friend who was teaching me so much that my parents hadn't even broached the subject about. I had a crush on Matt, who was showing more affection and attention to me than my own Dad and even Uncle Gerry seemed to be a nice guy.

I was a naïve, nearly twelve year old gay boy who fantasised about sex and they had got me into the situation that they must have wanted to do. They had led me there, but I had gone willingly, following my best mate and his Dad with the puppy love of an innocent.

Andrew Michelson

Chapter Nine – Friday 25th and Saturday 26th September

That felt like the perfect place to pause for thought as hopefully tomorrow, I will actually get through to the helpline and speak to someone. I have managed to get this far in my story, with only talking to my fellow writer and also with Tony, who has been a constant source of encouragement to me.

Looking back at that last chapter, as an adult it is obviously what was going on, but the eleven year old me didn't have a clue. I thought that Andy was like me, but a little more knowledgeable and that we were exploring and discovering things together.

It was only that night that I should have realised that Andy was already sexually active but my naivety kept me innocent. It had been some two months of work on Andy's part, and Matt's I suppose, to get me to the point where I was walking around their house naked, cuddling up to an equally naked Matt, while Andy was progressively taking my sexual learning from innocent touching and humping through clothes to actual, hard core sex. His little comments that he made, continually referencing his Dad or other men while we were engaged in sexual contact played constantly on my mind and he stepped it up once he knew of my crush on his Dad.

Now comes the real question that I asked myself when I started this journey, how much detail to go into and how

much to say? I've now read three or four other books where people have told what happened to them and they differ in how they tell their stories, from clinical detachment, through mild description to explicit descriptions of actions and emotions.

My own emotions vary as each day, even each hour passes. While I have been writing the history chapters, to this point, I remember through my rose tinted glasses about the enjoyment that I had with Andy. When I look back with my adult eyes, reading my comments, I realise how I had been manipulated. My mood swings back and forth from guilt to confusion, but at the moment, still lacking the anger of my author friend. Whether this comes in time, I'm not sure. Even before I've written about some of what happened, I know that I should feel anger.

Friday night was spent down my local. One of my friends, who is the person mainly responsible for most of my friends reading my other penname's books, had edited one of them in the past. I am toying with the idea of asking her to do the editing, rather than my normal editor who is a lady at my work. I know that she can keep secrets because I was finally let in on one by another friend about some problems with their son, only to find out that this lady had known for several weeks and had never let on.

Saturday came around with a hangover and memories of switching from lager to blue WKD. We had our first social night tonight, which we had been building up towards and with the added bonus of England playing Wales in the Rugby World Cup, it promised to be a great evening.

However, there was the subject of calling the helpline that reared its head. Perhaps I should have had a tin of beer for breakfast to take the edge of my headache and build up some Dutch courage because when it came to getting the number on my phone, I sat there looking at my phone, my finger hovering over the dial button.

Three times I got the number on screen and three times I bottled ringing. I don't know why. Maybe it is easier to "talk" to my laptop and type the words out rather than actually speaking to someone about what happened to me. By talking about it, by sharing it with another live human being, it would make it real again. I know that at some point, you will be reading this. At some point, I will publish this book. That makes it more real than a spoken conversation. But I can still decide not to publish.

So I am going to push on regardless and work through the events of my twelfth birthday and how it came to shape my life.

Andrew Michelson

Chapter Ten – Being Twelve

The following weekend was a change in routine. It was the weekend before my birthday, which was on the Thursday, but my Nan wouldn't be there for my birthday as she had booked to go abroad with four of her friends. My Granddad had died when I was nine so it was just her but she still went on holiday with the group of friends that they had when he was alive.

What this meant was that she wanted to take us all out for a meal before my birthday, rather than after it. Therefore, it was decided that my family party would be the weekend before. I was allowed to invite some of my friends and it was agreed that Andy and I would have the usual sleepover at our house on the Friday night, my party would be on the Saturday and he would go home after it, and we would have the meal out with my Nan on the Sunday.

Andy and I had to be careful though, as my sister still had an annoying habit of walking into my room despite my complaints to my parents about privacy. We got home from school and watched television after doing our homework. We had dinner and watched more television before finally being "sent" to bed. Making sure that my sister was in her own bed and less likely to interrupt us, we stripped but didn't get on my bed. Being an older house, the floorboards were a bit creaky and if there were two of us going at it on my bed, I'm sure it would have made my parents aware of what we were doing. Therefore we got

onto the foam mattress and spent some time kissing and touching each other before Andy gave me a "birthday blowjob" as he called it. I shot in his mouth but again wasn't expecting him not to have swallowed it because when he kissed me, I found that my ejaculate was still in his mouth. It was slimy but thought that I couldn't really complain as I was the one who had put it in his mouth after all. I reciprocated the blowjob and we settled down in our respective beds having got into our underwear just in case we had any visitors during the night.

The next day was the party and it was really manic. As I'd mentioned, my Dad's side of the family is huge and it seemed that everyone had come to the party. Much to my embarrassment, my parents put a video on of me. When I was younger, maybe five or six years of age, I had speech difficulties and had to see a speech therapist. During my treatment, my parents had given permission for one of the sessions to be recorded for training purposes. They had received a copy of it and had managed to get it transferred to VHS. So they must have taken great delight at my embarrassment of them putting it on in front of all of my relatives and friends.

Fortunately I survived it, got a shed load of cards and presents, mainly Star Wars figures bought courtesy of an Aunt who worked at Parker Toys who were commissioned in the UK to make them and of course, ate loads of party food and cake.

Andy went home after the party and on the Sunday, my Nan took us to a Beefeater steakhouse restaurant where we had the rare luxury of steak. I was even allowed to have three halves of cider with my meal and when we got home, we sat in the kitchen and my parents carried on the party weekend. My Mum got a bit drunk on Metaxa brandy and I was allowed to have some more alcohol, although having switched to white wine.

For the first time in my life, I got drunk. I was so ill that I thought I was going to die. I remember lying on the sofa

so that the room wouldn't hurt me as it spun and I was filling up one kitchen bowl with vomit as quickly as my Dad was emptying the other. I actually missed school the next day, my parents lying to the school about my sickness being a stomach bug. In a way, I supposed it was the truth as my stomach was doing ten to the dozen. Of course Andy giggled like mad when I told him why I hadn't been at school the following day and we were making plans for the following weekend. He pleaded with me to get my parents to agree to let me stop over on both the Friday and Saturday night, saying that his Dad wanted to take us to Wicksteed Park, which was like a smaller version of Alton Towers.

Thursday was my birthday and I received a few cards from school friends who hadn't been at my party as well as my presents and cards from my parents and sister. If I remember correctly, I got a new Leicester City football kit, complete with socks, and as a treat, dinner was a Chinese takeaway. I actually don't like the Chinese curries so I always had a quarter of chicken breast and chips. I bundled myself off to bed wondering how much fun Andy and I could have over the weekend and if we would all get naked again, giving me another chance to see Matt's body.

Friday was intolerably slow but as we got off the bus, we fairly ran to his house. Andy had told me that now his Dad knew about us watching the videos, he'd been able to go through them and found us a real good one to watch. I looked forward to see the naked men but was a little envious that it was the women who seemed to get to enjoy the men's dicks.

We threw our bags under the stairs as normal and went to Andy's room to get out of our school clothes. I'd learned the hard way about getting my school blazer crumpled. The stinging of my Mum's hand disappeared long after she had ironed it. We hung up our clothes and quickly shed our underwear. I no longer had any self-consciousness about being naked in front of my best

friend, even if I had a smaller willy than him. I knew that he wouldn't take the mickey out of me and, instead, he would normally play with it while I played with his. What better way to spend a Friday afternoon. We gave each other a quick kiss and grope before he reminded me about the video.

So we traipsed off to the lounge, via the kitchen to grab some drinks and crisps, before settling down to watch the film. It started off like the rest, with a bloke being on screen but when a second man came into the bedroom and there was no woman, I didn't understand to begin with. When they started kissing each other and touching, I was immediately interested. I asked Andy where the woman was and he giggled and said that this was a gay porno. I about shot there and then. I'd heard about men doing it with each other and now I was about to watch it happen. I couldn't believe it when one of them put his penis inside the other's bum hole and again, it was up to my best mate to explain about sex to me, telling me that was how two men did it. They seemed to really like it, even the man who was on the receiving end of it. Andy explained how there was a spot inside our bottoms that felt really good if you rubbed it. He reached down, underneath my testicles and rubbed my perineum. As he did, he gave me a blowjob and I had the best orgasm that I ever had. Once he finished, he kissed me, again with a mouthful of my sperm and he pushed it into my mouth, making me swallow it.

I quickly gave him one, which of course was what we were doing when his Dad walked into the room, having come home early from work. I quickly pulled off of Andy, but Matt just grinned at me and told me not to leave my best friend with blue balls. He said that he knew we had been playing around with each other for some time and that we should continue. I felt a little strange, going back down on my friend while his Dad stood there watching us,

but Andy took charge and was soon having his dry orgasm.

Matt got himself a drink and got naked and we both got our customary hugs. It felt really nice, having him squeeze my buttocks as he hugged me into him but we were then sat on the sofa, watching the end of the porno before moving on to normal television.

We went to bed, Andy having made sure that I stayed awake for a change and we got onto his bed and kissed each other. He was on top of me as normal but for a change, his hand wandered down my body and onto my hole. He said that he knew how to make me feel real good and wanted to do something special for my birthday. I said okay and before I knew what was happening, he had turned me over and with my now adult knowledge, he had lubed up his fingers. He rubbed my hole before pushing a finger into me. It must have felt okay as I didn't complain and he soon had two and then three fingers inside me. I remember it feeling really good but I didn't know where it was leading. I should have really, having watched two men butt fucking, but it was still a surprise when he put his penis against my hole and told me to push out like I was taking a dump.

He pushed into me, taking my virginity.

I was twelve years and one day old.

In later life, whenever the topic of when our first times was, I have mentioned to a few people about how young I was when I lost my virginity, people who know that I am gay. Some of them don't believe me. A couple of them think that I shagged a girl, I don't know why. Only half a dozen people know that I had anal sex with another lad but most do not realise what happened the next day.

Andy held me face down and had sex with me until he orgasmed. He'd put a pillow underneath me to raise up

my midsection so it was easier for him and, just like the experience with Dave and the rape game, the friction made me have my own climax. I remember making a mess on his pillow and apologising profusely, before he cleaned up the mess telling me that it was cool that I liked it so much.

I wasn't sure if I liked it or not, but knowing that I was gay, and having watched the gay men on the porno, I figured that it must be what gay men do. We went to sleep with Andy lying on top of me, holding me and I had never felt so loved in the world before.

The following morning was when my life changed forever.

I was twelve years and two days old.

That was the day that I truly lost my innocence.

Andy woke me up, babbling on about being excited about going to Wicksteed Park. Despite his Dad being well off, I think that he didn't get to go many places and he was more excited than I was about going. He asked if I liked what we did last night, and with my reluctant nod, he asked me if it was okay for him to do it to me again.

I had kind of liked it the night before, and wanting to keep him happy, as it meant that I would keep seeing Matt, I agreed that he could. We repeated the process of putting a rolled up pillow underneath me and he put some lube inside me and on him so that it was easy for him to penetrate me. He had me face down on his bed, my midsection raised and was, basically, fucking away on me when I felt a hand stroking my hair. I'd shut my eyes to concentrate on not feeling any pain but I knew instantly that the hand didn't belong to my friend.

Opening my eyes, I saw Matt's face on a level with my own. He was kneeling by the side of the bed and was stroking my hair with one hand while stroking my back

I'm not going to lie and pretend that it was fantastic and that I loved it. Despite all of my assertions that I wanted it, that I finally had what I desired, when he pushed his penis inside me it hurt like hell. I was crying, wanting him to stop but not wanting him to stop. I loved him so much that I wanted to please him so I gritted my teeth and let him do it to me despite the pain.

I remember the pain but I remember feeling his body on top of me. There was no way that I would have been able to get out from underneath him even if I had wanted to. His body weight forced me into the mattress, forced my dick onto the pillow and, despite the pain, I still got my orgasm. I can remember shuddering through it while he was on top of me and not being able to move.

I can't remember how long it took for him to climax inside me, but it seemed to last forever while being over far too quickly. He kissed me straight away afterwards, repeating that he thought I was so beautiful and Andy joined in. The two of them stroked my body and my ego, showering me with affection.

Matt made us breakfast while Andy helped me shower on unstable legs and, for once, we were dressed when we went downstairs to eat. Matt got changed and we spent several hours at Wicksteed Park. I don't remember how many rides that they had, but I remember eating a lot of junk food and going on several rollercoasters before we made the long journey home. I was tired out and fell asleep in the back of the car and was woken up by Matt carrying me out of the car. We all got naked and sat on the sofa watching whatever television was on. As usual Matt was in the middle but instead of his arms being around our shoulders, they were in our laps and he encouraged us to touch him as well. As this was just light touching, I was happy to do it, especially as he alternated kissing Andy and myself. I couldn't believe that he kissed his own son like that but I thought it looked nice and I

certainly was happy when it was my turn to be kissing Matt.

When Matt suggested that it was time for bed, I was a bit gutted to stop but he followed us upstairs and directed the pair of us into his bedroom rather than Andy's. We got onto his bed and I found myself in the middle of them. They took turns in kissing me while touching me all over before Matt told Andy it was time. I realised where it was leading and was sort of reluctant, having remembered how much it had hurt but when Matt reminded me that I must have enjoyed it because I'd cum when they did it before, I hesitated. When Andy touched my hole, I lost my resistance and let them turn me over.

Andy took me first, I assume to help prepare me for the larger penis of his Dad, but again, when Matt pushed into me, I struggled with the pain. While Matt was doing it to me, Andy would kiss me and masturbate me until I climaxed.

We went to sleep, the pair of them either side of me and I remember being in a state of confusion. On the one hand, it hurt when Matt was inside me, but on the other hand, they took time in making me feel special and loved, something that I didn't get at home.

I returned home on the Sunday sore but happy that I had made Matt happy, and with admonistrations that I shouldn't tell my parents about what we had got up to otherwise I wouldn't be able to come over and stay again. There was no way that I ever wanted that to happen and so my silence was bought for the first aspect of my abuse. I simply adored Matt too much and loved the friendship that I had with Andy and there was no way that I was going to ruin it.

I didn't know that it was wrong for a man to have sex with a boy. As mentioned previously, there were no stranger danger campaigns, there were no high profile abuse cases so it just didn't register to me that I shouldn't

be doing this stuff with Matt, and with Andy. By not saying anything, I suppose that I was complicit in my situation. I now know that, as a child, I should never had been put into that situation, but I still think that if that was all that happened to me, then I would have happily accepted it, even as an adult.

It is only now looking back with my adult eyes and rose tinted glasses removed that it was the start of the second phase of my grooming.

I remember being a bit quiet on the Sunday as I missed the closeness that I had just experienced. I think we must have visited one or more of my Aunts and Uncles, as that tended to be a routine on Sundays, but as soon as we got home, I went to my room under the pretence of having to do my homework. Nothing was said to me and, in my mind that allowed me to persuade myself that it was okay. In bed that night, I followed my usual routine but for a change, I did press my fingers against my anus. Now that it had time to recover, it did feel good and I obviously must have decided that, if they wanted to, I would let them do it again.

When I got to school on Monday, I could tell that Andy must have been nervous but as I greeted him as normal, he relaxed and we talked about normal stuff until he asked to talk to me alone at lunchtime. With the school housing nearly a thousand kids, they had to have a large area for all of us to play. They did rotate when we went in to eat, and the third years were allowed to leave school premises so there was probably around four to five hundred kids outside at any one time. We were only allowed inside if it was raining. There was a small playground that held around eighty to a hundred and then there was the large all weather play area. It was the size of three tennis courts and easily held a few hundred, as well as the field. This was larger than a football pitch and at the far end was a grassy bank which led into fields that belonged to a farmer.

while he penetrated me. The pain returned but Andy's words rang in my ears about it getting easier the more that I did it. How, I didn't know because it felt as bad as the first time but I gritted through it and didn't complain. After all, I was in love with Matt and wanted to do everything that he wanted me to. After he finished, they hugged and kissed me again, telling me once again how special and beautiful I was.

Over the next month or so, this was how the weekends would play out. I even started to miss the feeling when I was at home during the week and, being a very clever boy, I looked for ways to speed up the process of it not hurting me. I tried pushing the handle of my hairbrush inside me but it lacked the girth and that was when I saw the perfect implement. The six inch, weighted, third section of my pool cue. I measured it up in my mind and thought that it was only a little bit thinner than Matt's penis and it was about the same size in length. How I never got caught by my parents I will never know as each night, I would use my mouth to get it slippy before pushing it inside me. I think that my parents must have realised that I was ejaculating by that time as I always had enough tissues and hardly ever got a cold, but they couldn't have any idea about the real use for them, cleaning my new exercise toy.

Over time, my body got used to the invasion and I found that I did start to enjoy the feelings that they gave me. Each time that one of them would have sex with me, if the natural friction didn't bring me to a climax, then one of them would make sure that I did. Looking back with adult eyes, it was a calculated ploy on their part to reinforce what they were telling me. How could I not be enjoying it if I was having an orgasm while they did it to me? You only climax if you are enjoying the sex so I must be enjoying it. That is what they told me and what I believed. I loved the kissing and the touching, and grew to accept the sex as part of Matt's love for me.

It was a chance comment by me that I shouldn't have made that changed everything. One evening, I remember being cuddled by them after we had done it when I suddenly asked about why it was only me that was being made love to. Made love to. That is what Matt had told me that they were doing. Not sex. Love. Matt asked me what I meant when I felt brave enough by then to say that Andy had told me that they had been having love for a year but I hadn't seen them do it yet. Matt told me that when I was staying over, they wanted to show me how much they loved me which was why it was all about me. They had the other nights for Andy to be loved. However, Matt asked me if that is what I wanted to see and I nodded. I wanted to see if my friend enjoyed it as much as he kept telling me. Matt and Andy looked at each other and I saw Andy nod. Matt told me that the next time, I would be able to watch.

I should have kept my mouth shut and never asked. If I had, maybe it would have stayed like we had been doing. Somehow I doubt it, but maybe it would have. In a way, it's my fault although I know everyone will tell me it wasn't as I shouldn't have been in that situation anyway.

Chapter Eleven – Tuesday 29th September

It's amazing that, once you start something, despite your fears and worries about it, how quickly things go. About a week ago, I decided to give the chapters a title. Each of the historical chapters where easy enough, as they were named for the part of my life that I was about to describe whereas these chapters are named for the date that I am typing them. It was taking me two to three weeks at the beginning but now, I am finding myself writing and reviewing a chapter in the space of a couple of days. Whether or not it is because I am finding it easier to express myself and my thoughts, or that now I have reached the point where the sexual abuse has started and there is no more working to that point, I am not sure. All that I know is that I am going to have to be careful from here on in.

Rereading the last part of chapter ten, I still find myself blaming myself in part for what happened to me. Even leading up to that point, if I had told someone, a teacher, a policeman, my parents… it would have stopped before it got past the point that it did. I still look back on the history so far and think about how much I loved Matt at that time, despite or perhaps because of what he was doing to me. I knew that when a man and a woman loved each other, they made love and with Matt continually telling me about how much he loved me and how special I was, I

guess that I thought it was what we were supposed to do. Once I had got used to the pain of penetration, it didn't feel so bad and both Matt and Andy were at pains, pardon the pun, to tell me how special I was and how much I obviously enjoyed it.

This is where my head is a little messed up, I guess, because my rose tinted memories were that I did enjoy it. It is only now, looking back with clear, adult eyes that I realise how easily I allowed myself to be groomed by them.

I mentioned at the end of chapter ten about how I also blame myself for the abuse to be taken to the next level. I know that I shouldn't blame myself, but a part of me can't help it. By asking about Andy, it opened the door, unknown at that time, for the abuse to go further. I can't help now but think that Andy was totally complicit with it, but also wonder if he was as much of a victim as I was. After all, he had been used sexually for over twelve months before me, but he played a large role in introducing me to sex. I suppose that he was probably coerced into it by his Dad and that I shouldn't blame him at all, and in truth, I don't.

The blame has to lie with the adults but still... I still haven't got to a point where I am having the same feelings of anger as my friend. I feel guilty about that but also keep getting told not to feel guilty about it.

Tony has now read the first nine chapters and, again has offered me words of support. I asked him about how he felt, as I had never been into this much detail with him before. All that he knew about me was that I was twelve when I had sex with my friend and that his Dad joined in. He knew nothing about the previous history, he knew nothing about the level of preparation that they went to and he knew nothing about what I am about to continue writing. He told me that the way I explained my enjoyable experiences was good but that he also felt very angry about how I had been manipulated. He said that I was very

brave in exploring my past and writing it down, baring my soul.

My author friend also reiterated that. So far, she has only read chapter one and heard the snippets of chapter two. She wants to read the complete story, even if she has to wait to buy it. I told her that I might print out some more and let her have it at the next writers group, but at the same time, it would be very embarrassing for me the next time that I saw her. After all, I am going into a lot of personal details and feelings. I won't ever get to meet you, the reader, so this is anonymous, but for her, well, she will see me on a regular basis.

Anyway, I think that I am blathering on to hold off writing the next chapter for fear of how my emotions will be but, if I don't write it, then I will never get past it.

Again, before you pass judgement on what you are about to read, remember that I was a young boy, finally happy that I had people to talk to about being queer, as they called it back in the early eighties, and that I thought that I was in love with a hunk of a man, who I would do anything to keep his affection.

Andrew Michelson

Chapter Twelve – The Next Level

It turned out not to be the next weekend that we got to spend the next sleepover. It was half term and my parents wanted to go and visit some relatives that we had in Manchester. I was disappointed that I would miss out on seeing Matt and Andy but the lure of going to Old Trafford more than made up for it. Although now being a Leicester City supporter, I had actually been a Manchester United fan until the age of ten, when my Dad took me to see my first live game. It had been at Filbert Street and I was a convert from then on in. So I still had a soft spot for Manchester United and was delighted when they won. I remember being thrilled to see Stevie Coppell playing because he was my favourite player at the time, a winger who also played for England.

We spent the weekend up at our relatives... I can't remember the exact connection. I think it was the sister to my uncle who had married my Dads sister... if that all makes sense? So it was my Dads brother in law's sister and family. All very complicated. All that I remember, other than the football, was sleeping on a very uncomfortable camp bed for three nights and I was pleased to get home for more than that reason. The camp bed was also in the room that my parents were sleeping in so I had no privacy at night-time. I had got use to sleeping naked, unknown to my parents, so I had to wear shorts to sleep in as well as not being able to play with myself, like I normally did. Three nights and four days when you are a

sexually active twelve year old is a long time. A very long time.

So it wasn't too disappointing to me when we got home. I rang Andy almost as soon as I'd thrown all of my dirty clothes in the laundry bin, only for there to be no reply. I tried ringing him several times over the next few days but no-one answered.

To take my mind off him, I agreed to "play" with the girl who lived next door. She was a few years younger than me and Portuguese. Her Poppa was the head waiter in the restaurant at the posh hotel that we had in town and I got the feeling that she didn't really have many friends. I never saw her have any over and occasionally, when I wasn't with Andy, I would go to her house and play board games.

I remember that it was her that instigated it, simply because I was gay and wouldn't have made a move on her, but we did kiss. I must have taken the role of the older brother to her, and her parents, so I felt it only right that I acted like my sister had with me, when Isabella asked if I'd kissed a girl before. I showed her how to kiss properly but it didn't go any further than that. I simply wasn't interested in her in that way, and I am sure that she was probably disappointed that I didn't. Bit vain of me, I guess, but looking back at my photographs from that age, I was a good looking kid, slim and sporty and, I hope, a nice personality to boot.

We went back to school after the week long break and Andy explained that his Dad, his Uncle and him had gone to visit some of their friends in the Lake District. Understandable I guess because my parents had done the same, well, visiting relatives anyway. We asked what each of us had got up to and I was a little pleased I guess when he was jealous of me going to the football match. He explained that they had been to a cottage on one of the lakes and they had been swimming in the lake, which was cold he giggled, and played a lot of outdoor games. I was

dying to ask him if he had sex but thought that if there were other people there, then his privacy was probably at the same level of mine.

School work had started picking up pace as we only had a few weeks before the end of year exams so we did get our heads down. Mainly. I did get my head in the wrong place during that term. There was a boy who I sat next to in Maths called Pete. We were normally friends and so I cannot remember why we fell out, but we did, and in true High School fashion, our so called friends egged us on to have a fight at break time. We arranged to meet at the back of the English block, away from the prying eyes of teachers and when break time came around, I walked around the block to meet up with my friend to try to talk him out of the fight. I found out afterwards that he had gone there with similar thoughts but when I turned the corner and saw him, there was a crowd of around fifty or so other pupils.

Fights at school in my day were a major event. As soon as one was organised, word spread through the student underground grapevine and how it never got to the attention of the teachers before the fights started, I have no idea. Unless the teachers worked on the premise that boys needed to let off steam and would arrive a few minutes into the fight before any major damage was inflicted. So Pete and I looked at each other knowing that neither of us could back down or we would lose face with our peers. It wasn't a fight in the true sense of the word. He grabbed me around the neck and I grabbed his body trying to free myself. We moved around like a rolling maul in rugby, encircled by the pack that landed more punches on the two of us than we threw ourselves. The word "teacher" was shouted and everyone split, including Pete and myself, for fear of detention and the slipper was more of a deterrent than losing face. We ended up hiding around by the bike sheds, breathing hard from the sprint

away and ended up laughing at the ridiculous situation that we'd got ourselves into.

He'd escaped with a couple of bruises on his legs where he'd been kicked by the crowd but I'd managed to catch a stray punch on my eye. It turned into a black eye, which did actually improve my street cred with my fellow peers.

Of course, my Mum gave me a roasting for getting in a fight, while I think my Dad was secretly pleased that I had done. It showed that I was tough and not willing to back down, something that he would have been proud of. I didn't tell him that I hadn't thrown a single punch during the fight.

When the Friday came around and I went back with Andy to his house, my eye was still painful to touch. It had gone a purple and yellow colour and I was worried that I would look ugly to Matt and that he might not want to kiss me this time. I hadn't seen him for two weeks, a long time when you are that young. I saw his car in the driveway and figured that he must have taken time off again to make this extra special.

We got in, shouted a hello to his Dad and followed our normal routine. School bags chucked under the stairs. School clothes removed and neatly hung up. A quick grope of each others' bits before stripping and heading back downstairs. The thought that I was going to get to see Matt and Andy make love had been playing on my mind as the week had drawn to an end and now it was nearly here, I was very excited.

We walked into the lounge and I was struck by two differences to the norm. Firstly, there was a big mattress in the middle of the lounge floor. It had a white sheet over it, one of those sheets that fitted around it rather than had to be tucked in. It looked to be about the size of Matts' bed and I found out later that it was from the third bedroom, which was a guest room.

The second difference to the norm was that Uncle Gerry was in the room. This wasn't what I was expecting and I

thought that my dreams of watching Andy and Matt making love and then me joining in afterwards had gone up in smoke. Now I was a smart lad, but sometimes I guess I lacked common sense when presented with situations out of the norm. Why would there be a mattress in the lounge if we weren't going to use it, and of course, why would they both be naked as well?

Andy hugged and kissed his Dad before doing the same to his Uncle. Matt pulled me in for a hug and kiss and I struggled as he kissed me fully on the mouth. I remember him asking what was wrong and I pointed to Gerry, saying something about not letting him know. Matt smiled and told me not to worry and maybe I should go and greet Uncle Gerry as well. I slowly walked over, feeling self conscious for the first time in a long time because I was erect in front of him but Gerry just pulled me towards him. He had knelt down to greet Andy and had remained in that position so that he was at the same height as me. He put a hand on the back of my head and kissed me, just like Matt and Andy did, while his rubbed his other hand over my back and buttocks.

I felt uncomfortable letting him do it but Matt had told me to go and greet him so I stood there and let him molest me, basically. He finally stopped kissing me and had a big smile on his face. I moved back away from him, to the safety of the side of Matt and wrapped and arm around my crush's waist.

We sat down, with Andy on his Uncle's lap and Matt, for the first time, pulled me up and onto his lap, and we were asked about Andy's day and my week. Matt made a big fuss over my blackened eye but all the way through the conversation, their hands were touching us.

I was squirming, not used to being touched in front of another man but Andy acted like it was nothing new. Matt kept kissing me on the top of my head, my cheek and my mouth before he said that it was time that I watched how

much Andy liked being made love to. Gerry and Andy stood up and Gerry placed Andy on the mattress.

Andy got on his hands and knees and Gerry pushed his fingers inside his anus. I knew that you had to do that otherwise it would hurt. Gerry soon penetrated Andy and I watched as he made love to him. All of the time that this was happening, Matt was stroking me and petting me. For once, I didn't like it when he wanted to kiss me, mainly because it meant that my eyes were looking up at him rather than at Andy and Gerry.

When they finished, I could feel Matt's erection poking against my bottom. Watching Andy and Gerry, as well as Matts' constant touching meant that I was erect as well. Matt stood and lifted me up and put me on the mattress, in place of Andy and Gerry who had taken a seat on the sofa. I remember saying that I didn't want to do it in front of Gerry, but Matt chided me, telling me that I had just watched him with Andy and it would be unfair if we didn't share our love with them.

I couldn't argue with his logic at that time and so, I willingly let him put me in the same position as Andy had been in. This was new for me as I was always lying face down before. I had got used to Matt putting his fingers inside me, as well as my own exercises at getting myself used to being penetrated and it wasn't long before Matt made love to me in front of the other two. I remember feeling funny because I didn't have the pillow underneath my groin and it was flopping about, until Matt took it in his hand.

He masturbated me while he made love to me and, as always, succeeded in making me climax before he had his. He pulled out and I always remember feeling empty after he did. Even now, as an adult, I hate that part about sex. When you are the bottom in the coupling, there is such an intimacy about having your partner's penis inside you, that when it is removed, it literally leaves a hole.

I thought that would be that, but Andy got up and took Matts' place behind me. I should have known because every time we made love, both of them did it to me so why would this be any different?

Gerry and Matt were making comments while Andy did it, mainly to do with how hot and sexy it looked and how cute and beautiful we were. Comments aimed at making us feel better, I suppose, and I guess it worked. Andy wasn't doing what Matt had done so I wasn't really getting my feelings, something that the other two must have noticed. Gerry got on his knees by the side of me and took me in his hand. It was the first time that he touched me there, the first time someone other than Matt or Andy touched me in what I knew to be a sexual nature. He was obviously experienced because he took me to my orgasm.

When Andy finished, I sort of flopped down on the mattress. I thought that this time, that would be it for now but I was wrong. Gerry got behind me and lifted my mid-section up. As I had just been done by the other two, I guess he thought there was no need to do anything other than push himself inside me.

I remember saying that I didn't want him to do it, that I loved Matt and only wanted him to make love to me. Matt reminded me that I let Andy do it to me, and besides, Gerry was family and we all loved Gerry and he loved us as well. I wanted to argue more but it was already too late. Matt stroked my back and hair and told me how much he loved me, how special I was and how he really wanted me to let Gerry show me his love as well. But if I wanted Gerry to stop, then he would but it would mean that I couldn't join in with them any longer.

That was the nail in the coffin. He knew that I loved him and would do almost anything for him and he used it against me. I lay on the mattress and allowed Gerry to have sex with me. Writing this, I won't call it making love because it wasn't. I knew that I didn't love Gerry, I

liked him, but I didn't love him like I loved Matt, and I know now that I was just a sex object to Gerry.

When he finished, he pulled me on to his lap on the sofa and I finally got my wish of watching Andy and Matt make love. Gerry was touching and kissing me throughout as they worked on getting me used to him touching me, I suppose.

We watched television and had dinner and remained naked throughout the evening. Andy and I were passed between the two, sitting on their laps, letting them kiss and fondle us before Gerry said it was time for him to leave. He got dressed and gave Andy a big kiss and a hug, before turning to me. I knew that I wouldn't get away with anything less so I went to him and kissed him as well. He pulled out a five pound note and gave it to me saying that I was an extra special boy and deserved a treat.

Five pounds in those days was a huge amount to a twelve year old boy and I thanked him. He ruffled my hair and the second part of my silence had just been bought, literally. Gerry said something about the next time and waved goodbye.

We sat on the sofa, Matt in the middle as always but this time, we were perched on each of his legs. He rubbed our stomachs and asked if we'd enjoyed ourselves. I didn't want to upset him so I said that I had. After all, Matt had made me feel good again, and we had done a lot of kissing. I'd seen him and Andy make love but the only part that I hadn't been wanting was what Gerry had done. Matt asked if Gerry had hurt me at all or made me feel special. Being a mainly truthful lad, I said he hadn't hurt me so Matt said that he must have made me feel special.

For once, when we went to bed, I was placed on the outside and I watched them make love again before they hugged me and we went to sleep.

Chapter Thirteen – Tuesday 29th September part two

Having three days off work to use up holiday can really help to concentrate your mind. Having written and reread the last chapter, I think that this is where I am supposed to start getting angry. That night, which was supposed to have been a special time when I saw Andy be made love to for the first time, turned into what I suppose you can only call a group orgy.

I had never thought about Gerry making love to me, I didn't love him and even though I had seen him naked, it was more curiosity rather than attraction. Of course, I wasn't to know that both Matt and Gerry had been having sex with Andy all of that time and that they were using my crush on Matt and my curiosity about Andy to have brought me up to the point where Gerry could join in.

Looking back through the previous chapters, and yes, I am doing a lot of rereads to ensure that I have remembered things correctly, each step of my sexual awakening was controlled, never pushing me too far too quickly where there would be a risk of me telling someone about it. Each step, it was reinforced into me that I was loved, that I was special and beautiful and that, because I was having my climax, that I was enjoying it. I even did have my climax that first time with Gerry, which

just further told the twelve year old me that they must be right.

With all of what happened to me, I am positive that it played a huge percentage of my sexual development. Not my sexual orientation, because that is born into you. You can fight against it, pretend it isn't there, lie to yourself and everyone else. I was an expert at that for many years of my adult life, pretending to be straight, pretending that this never happened to me but God, I was miserable in private. I knew that I liked men, that I do like men and that I want men to use me sexually.

No, the sexual development that I am talking about is what role you take with your partner, what fuels your desires and fantasies. Some people who have very early sexual experiences with their peers cannot lose that desire for sex with partners of that age, even after they grow up. This is not me. Despite Andy being a huge role in my sexual development, it was always Matt that I fixed my fantasies on. This has led me to crave contact with older men, men who can play the dominant father figure role. It is getting more difficult as I get older myself but fortunately, men's libidos keep going until late in life.

I have recently met up with a guy called Dave who fits into all of the desires that I need. He is sixty seven, some twenty three years older than me, and very much a 'Daddy' figure. Before you think that I had thoughts about my own Dad, I didn't. I am simply using the terms that fit. Dad/Son is one term used for the meets where there is a significant age gap between the two. He likes to kiss and cuddle with me, taking me back to Matt, and has no qualms about using his fingers. He doesn't yet know about my past, but I have promised to tell him the next time we meet. That hasn't been arranged yet, but in a way, I am looking forward to it.

Another part of my development is that, while I like the intimacy of a one on one, I also like being involved with

groups. This can only have come from what happened to me, once Gerry was introduced into the mix.

As I said before, these random thoughts that I am putting down on paper are highly embarrassing when I think about the people who will read this, but I want to get over why I feel like I do, why I have never told anyone in authority about what happened to me, why I am struggling to feel the anger.

A lot of what happened to me forged my future sexual experiences which, when I threw off the shackles of pretending to be straight, have been extremely enjoyable.

Well, today has been a tough but productive day. I have written approaching five thousand words and written down about the first time that I was, for want of a better word, raped. There... I have finally said the word. The definition of rape is to forcibly make someone have sexual intercourse against their will. While I was not threatened with violence, Matt had used the threat of not being able to do anything with him again, something that he banked on me wanting to avoid. Therefore I went against my own wishes to have sex with someone that I didn't want to.

So I will leave my writing here for today and I will go for some Dutch courage. Tonight is one of the two sessions with the male volunteer so maybe, if I go for a couple of drinks early, I will have the nerve to ring them and speak with them before continuing.

Andrew Michelson

Chapter Fourteen – Summer Holidays

Over the next few weeks, Gerry became a somewhat part-time addition to our weekends. He didn't come over every weekend, probably once every two or three weeks, and when he did, it was sometimes on the Friday evening leaving before we went to bed, or sometimes he would stay over.

Whenever he did come over though, it was always the same. After we got naked, Andy and I would be passed from one to the other, sitting in their laps, letting them play with us and us fondling them while we kissed. Andy and I would also be made to kiss and touch each other while they watched. We both were soon performing oral sex on them as well, something that I didn't like. I understand now why Andy used to keep my ejaculate in his mouth after he'd blown me and made me swallow it. He was getting me ready for when Matt and Gerry would ejaculate in my mouth.

The two of them had different styles. Whether Matt was playing the "good cop" to Gerrys' "bad cop" I am not sure. Looking back it may have been just another ploy of theirs to keep me wanting to do anything to please Matt, but at the time, I fell for it whatever it was. Gerry was quite aggressive while Matt took his time with me, but when he was with Andy, he was equally as aggressive. By aggressive, I don't mean hitting or anything, but with me he was gentle, taking his time

whereas Gerry, I think, was just using us as a receptacle for his penis.

On the nights that he did stay over, the four of us would all be together in Matt's bed, again with Andy and I being exchanged between them but it always ended with Matt cuddling with me as we went to sleep.

I began to withdraw slightly, not really liking the fact that I was being shared with Gerry, as I only wanted to be with Matt but Matts' continual expression of love for me, and assertion that we were all one big family of love, kept me quiet. Gerry did continue to give me pocket money, not necessarily a five pound note, but in a way, I liked the extra money and, I suppose, as I thought that I kind of liked the feelings he gave me, I kept the secret.

When the summer holidays came around, Matt made arrangements with my parents for the sleepovers to continue. My parents had got used to me being over there by then, I guess, and with one less mouth to feed for around a week every month, I am sure they noticed the difference in their money as well.

The subject of holidays came up and that year, I think my family and I went to a caravan in South Devon. Dawlish Warren I think it was, and my over-riding memories of it were that my sister was less than impressed that her bed, like mine, was the converted sofa in the lounge which she had to share with me. Separate beds, but the same room. The lights were gas powered and I can still remember the smell of them, and our caravan was right next to the train line that ran the other side of the fence of the caravan park. There was a regular train in the early hours of the morning which always woke me up.

Of course, being in such close quarters and not having a lot of hot water to spend extra time in the shower, I went a whole week without touching myself sexually. It probably did me good as it allowed my body to recover from the constant sex that it was getting each weekend,

but I remember ringing Andy as soon as we got home and begging to arrange a sleepover. Matt was only too happy and I spent two days at theirs and it was just the three of us. I liked it when it was just the three as it was unhurried and gentle.

That's when Matt asked if I wanted to go on holiday with them. Of course I said yes, without even thinking about it. Matt spoke to my parents, who again put up a complaint about how much money it would cost, only for Matt to tell them that if me being there made Andy happy, then he was happy to pay to keep his son happy. Or something like that. However, my parents did give him some money, I don't know how much but I am sure it wouldn't have covered the complete holiday. Matt took it with a little fuss but I guess it was a pride thing for my parents.

Details were exchanged and I was under threat from my Mum to do whatever Matt told me to and not to misbehave. I was also to ring them when I got there.

Where was there? There was where I fully lost my innocence. It had been slowly eroded away over the course of six months, from that first hump of the rape game, through Andys' slow but sure seduction and education of me, to losing my virginity first to him and then to Matt, until finally I was a willing if reluctant partner to the foursomes that included Gerry.

When Matt picked me up the following weekend, I was a little deflated to see Gerry in the front of the car and I realised that my dreams of a comfortable holiday with just Matt and Andy weren't going to happen. If I only knew that worse was to follow, I probably wouldn't have gone. During the journey to the Lake District, Gerry kept making crude comments about how much fun we were going to have, how he hoped that the weather was good so that we would spend the entire week naked and how much he was looking forward to seeing me in action again.

I felt uncomfortable about him talking like that, as if I was a performer for him, but Andy just rubbed me and told me that I would really enjoy the week. He was so enthusiastic that I couldn't help but be infected by him and I put my worries to the side. I shouldn't have really.

We finally got the cottage, having driven for it seemed hours down a winding road and pulled up next to the building. It looked like one of the cottages that you see in the olden paintings or pictures, but it was obviously well kept. Matt told me that it belongs to a couple of friends and that they liked it here because it was very secluded. It looked out onto one of the bigger lakes, I can't remember which and they said that there wasn't another house or cottage within a few miles.

We unloaded the car and unpacked our clothes. There were three bedrooms and they put my clothes in with Andy's while Matt and Gerry put theirs in a second room. We had a snack for lunch before Matt announced that we were going for a swim. I went to get my swimming trunks but the others just laughed and said that we were skinny dipping. Having been naked with them so often, amongst other things, I had no qualms about shedding my clothes after being told that no-one would be able to see us. We went swimming and generally messed around, throwing a ball to each other and Andy and I getting onto the shoulders of Matt and Gerry to try to push each other off. It was fun, but I was acutely aware of our bodies being pressed together.

When the game of tag started, that's when the fun turned. There was a lot of grabbing and groping, myself included, but when Gerry pressed a finger inside me, I knew that the games had stopped. I knew that it would do no good to complain, so I just let him finger me before he had sex with me. In the lake. I remember that this was the first time that I didn't climax when he had sex with me because no-one was touching my penis. Gerry had turned me to face him and was holding me up,

pushing me up and down on him. When it was over, I saw that Matt had been doing the same to Andy. Gerry tried to kiss me, but for once I avoided it, saying I needed to go to the toilet. He laughed and said just to let it go in the lake, but I said it wasn't a wee.

We all got out and I ran to the toilet and pretended to go for a dump. I used the time to get my thoughts together but I guess that I knew that this holiday was mainly going to be about them having sex with us. To be honest, it must have seemed to me that it was the same as the sleepovers, just longer and in a different place, which is why when I rang home, I just said that everything was fine and that we had been swimming already. It felt naughty talking to my Mum while I was standing naked, something that Andy had made a joke about before I rang her. He had got me hard so I was trying not to think about anything to do with sex while I was talking to her.

That night was a first for me. After we had done the usual cuddling and kissing in the lounge, no television because of no aerial, Andy and Gerry went into the room that had been put aside for us boys while Matt took me into the adults room. This was what I had wanted, what I had dreamed about. I had a whole evening alone with Matt. He made me feel so special and I was so happy to finally have him to myself. He told me that if I wanted, we could spend more nights where it was just the two of us, but it would mean that some nights, I would have to be with others as well. Thinking that he meant Gerry and Andy, I said okay, but only if we could spend nights together at least once every other sleepover. He kissed me a lot after that.

Unknown to me, he had just bought my silence for a third time, with the promise of being alone with him at the expense of giving myself away at other times. I was to discover this on this very holiday.

The next day came around far too quickly for me and I was surprised that, after Matt had showered me, we got dressed. We actually went hiking! Being in the Lake District meant that there were lots of paths around the lakes and indeed up hills. I remember being very scared on one such trek which led us across a narrow path that had a long drop off but all in all, it was okay. Being a fit lad, I easily kept up with the others.

We got back towards the end of the afternoon and someone suggested that we go for a swim to wash off, rather than shower. So we stripped off and got in the lake. There wasn't as much horseplay because I think that Andy and I were tired from the walking but there was still a fair amount of touching. I can't remember which of the men it was but I do remember one of them masturbating me in the lake until I climaxed. It felt weird, doing that underwater. I'd never done it before like that.

That evening, after dinner, Gerry took me to the same bedroom that he had taken Andy the night before, while Andy went with Matt. This was my first time alone with him and it was an experience that I didn't relish. He wasn't at all gentle, although he never hit me or anything. Not even a spank. He just put me on the bed and got me ready while I had to perform oral sex on him to get him ready. Then he put me on my back and held my legs up and did it. Again, I failed to climax on that first time but he did make sure that I did climax during the rest of the evening. He was reinforcing the "if you get your orgasm then you obviously enjoy it" idea that they planted in my head.

I remember nearly crying at one point when he did go too hard, which he must have realised as he did go a little easier, but there certainly wasn't much tenderness in him. He did make me kiss him during one of the positions that he put me in, one which became the normal one whenever I was with him. He would sit on the bed and

make me straddle his lap, facing him. I would then have to lower myself onto him and basically be the one who made the action. This let him kiss me while we did it as well as give him easy access to be able to masturbate me, but looking back, I think that the main reason for that particular position was that it made it that it was me who was doing it, and if it was me doing it, then I must like it. In a way, I did grow to prefer that position with Gerry because it did let me control the sex to a point... he did sometimes take hold of my waist and make me go faster or harder, but it was much better than when he was in total charge.

He did cuddle with me when we went to sleep, eventually, but there were no special words of love like I got from Matt. The next day, when asked by Matt, I think that he knew that I hadn't really enjoyed but when asked if I was okay and would continue, I just smiled and said yes, knowing that it was the only way to get my special alone time with him.

Looking back with my adult eyes, that night with Gerry was a pivotal night for them. They had deliberately taken me out of my comfort zone of having Matt there and Gerry hadn't been all loving and tender. When I didn't complain about it, it signalled to them that I would let it continue.

That day, we were swimming in the lake and playing around outside when two men arrived at the cottage in a car. I remember that Matt was giving me a piggy back at the time, because I liked the feeling of my groin being trapped between my body and his. I thought that we would all run inside and hide or get dressed or something, but Matt just walked up to them with me still naked on his back. He said hello to them before putting me on the ground and telling me to give them a hug. I was very embarrassed because I was sporting an erection, having been rubbing it on Matts' back but they didn't

hold back. Both of them hugged me tight and both of them touched my bottom while doing it.

Joe and George were their names and it was their cottage that we were staying at. They lived together, but this was way before same sex marriage was legal, so they used the excuse of house sharing to anyone who asked. Matt explained that they would be joining us for a few days and I shivered under the look that they were giving me. I was about to say something when Andy came running up and jumped into Joe's arms and kissed him. I stood and watched as my friend was molested in front of me before he was passed onto George who did the same.

Matt and I led the way into the cottage where they put their bags in the third bedroom, which was the master bedroom. We were sat in the lounge, in our usual position of Andy on Gerrys' lap and me on Matt's, when the two men came back out. Both were naked and both had erections. I guess that they were around Matt's age, although Joe could have been older as his hair was grey. He was a bit podgy and a bit shorter than Matt. George wasn't very nice to look at, at all. He was around the same size as Gerry in height but he was fat. His belly hung low and I remember that he smelled of sweat.

They said something about how they'd been looking forward to meeting me, and to see Andy again and I realised now that these were the friends that Andy had been visiting at Easter. My initial thoughts back then about if Andy had been having sex came back to haunt me as they took their seats.

If I had any doubts that Matt meant what he had said about sharing me with other men, they vanished completely in the next three days. There were things that we did that I must have blocked from my memory, and it is only now that I am really trying to remember things that they are resurfacing. This is part of why I was reluctant to begin remembering, but needed to do it. This is the part of my story where I will change from

remembering the nice, fun times that I remember to exploring some of the bad.

Those three days, the four of them did a lot of things to Andy and me. Things that I will not go into details about but I am remembering being on my knees between their legs and having my anus penetrated a lot by both fingers and penises. It seemed to be never ending but they managed to keep going. They would masturbate Andy and me, making it into a race as to who would climax first as well as other times making it a competition as to who would last the longest. They would have their own competitions as to who could be the first to ejaculate inside us. Apparently this is what they had done in the past, but with it only being Andy involved, they would take turns. With me added into the mix, they would put us facing each other so that we could watch each other being abused and they would race each other.

Andy and I would also have to make out with each other while they rested and watched. I didn't mind that because it was generally just kissing and touching although Andy would also make love to me. Looking back, I was never allowed to penetrate Andy, which I think is why I am now such a submissive bottom with my partners. I grew up thinking that I could only achieve a climax by another's hand while I was being penetrated.

The evenings were the worst for those three nights. As there were four of them, they paired off and took one each of Andy and me to bed. That was the first time that I was used at both ends at the same time. Joe and Gerry were the ones who did it and I remember thinking that I would be sick when I was first presented with a penis to lick that had been inside my anus.

Those three days wasn't all sex, I know I am making it seem like it. We did do normal things, like go hiking and walk the nature trails but there was a lot of sex. On the day that they left, Matt took me into one of the rooms that night and spent the "special time" with me as we

would call it. He did everything that I liked, kissing and cuddling, playing with my hole and making love to me slowly and gently. Again, looking back, he was taking the first opportunity to remind me what I would be missing if I decided that I didn't want to carry on with the others.

For the rest of the summer holidays, we alternated between Andy coming over to our house for the day and me going to his at the weekends. Each time that Gerry was there, we would all play together before we went to bed but it was Matt that I went with, while Andy and Gerry went to Andys' room.

I thought that I could live with it, putting up with Gerry while enjoying the special times with Matt but when he approached my parents about going away for a week again, just before the end of the holidays, I wasn't that enthusiastic. My parents were delighted that I would be getting another week away, less for them to spend on me without feeling guilty, I guess.

We got to the cottage and this time, Joe and George were already there. They stayed for the whole week and Andy and I were used sexually throughout. Matt made sure that I had a couple of nights alone with him, and I remember wondering how Andy felt about having to sleep with three of them while I was alone with his Dad. I can remember the noises that came from that room on those nights and Andy always looked tired the next day. Again, we did do normal things as well, but my over-riding recollections at this time are about the sex, as that is what I am concentrating on remembering. They did what they did to us before, swapping us between them and holding their competitions. I guess being a competitive lad, that led me into some type of enjoyment or at least acceptance of it, but it was mainly the time spent alone with Matt that kept me co-operative.

School came around again and this time, we were second years. I was a year older than the first time I sat next to Andy on that fateful day and my life had changed

dramatically. I look back now and wonder what would have happened in my life if I had chosen to sit next to one of the girls but I guess I'll never know.

Andrew Michelson

Chapter Fifteen – Sunday 4th October

That chapter was difficult to write. Looking back, I can now see how much they relied on my infatuation of Matt, using it over and over to ensure my co-operation. At the time, I would have done anything that he asked me to, and I did.

That first holiday away with them was the ultimate turning point of it all. I had not told anyone. I had allowed them to do it. I even went back that second time and let it happen all over again.

This is the part where I know that I am supposed to get angry about what happened and in a way, I am. But I feel more anger at myself, which I know that I shouldn't as I was just a young boy. I am also still, in part, remembering how special Matt made me feel and wanting to remember those nice, enjoyable times rather than focusing on the bad.

I guess this is why I really should speak to the helpline, to talk through it all with someone who has either been through it themselves, or to arrange the counselling that they offer. But I don't want to switch everything about in my head, even if it is the "right" thing to do.

Does that make sense? Preferring to blinker myself might not be the professional opinion but for me, it still seems like the best solution. After all, this happened some three decades ago so there isn't a great deal that I can do about the past.

All I can think about is the present and the future and how I go forward. I have my unconscious coping strategies in place, the guys from the website who I use for my own fulfilment as much as they use my body for theirs. When I'm in bed alone, which is most nights, my sexual fulfilment comes by pretending to be held down by a man, my pillow rolled underneath me and one of my dildos up inside me, giving me the release that I need.

Chapter Sixteen – The Next Fourteen Months

After we went back to school, things settled back into the normal routine. Well, if you can call what was happening normal. The sleepovers continued most weekends and the sex continued as well. Gerrys' presence stepped up to being there virtually every time but, as before, Matt made sure that I had my "special time" with him as often as possible.

By now, I must have got used to what was happening as I found myself waiting for the weekends to arrive. Embarrassingly to admit, when I was at home during the week, the end of the pool cue was being put to regular use as a makeshift dildo, although I didn't know what it was called or anything like that at the time. I just knew that it felt nearly as good as the real thing.

When half term approached, the offer of the holiday came around and, as before, my parents were only too happy and willing to let me go. Joe and George were there again and, as before, they used Andy and I for their pleasure. I suppose that isn't exactly true because we did get pleasure ourselves from it, but of course, they shouldn't really have been doing what they were doing with us.

Without repeating myself over and over, this was the course of the next twelve months. Weekends were mainly Matt, Gerry, Andy and myself, and during a

school holiday, they took me to the cottage where Joe and George would join us.

I think that I had become desensitised to the whole thing because I cannot remember complaining to Matt after the first couple of holidays. It had just become a part of the routine that they had built up around me.

Looking back and remembering, I can still feel the weight of George when he was on top of me, but I am guessing that because it pushed me into the mattress, I got my feelings from the friction just like before. As I've said before, even to this day, it remains one of my favourite positions, either solo with a pillow underneath me, or if I am with a partner. To feel myself with no control of my body, not being able to move while I am pushed into the mattress is definitely a result of what happened to me.

Andy had his thirteenth birthday in the October of the first year, and it wasn't long after that he had his first wet climax. I remember that afterwards, it would become a regular thing for us to perform a sixty nine position in front of them and trade kisses afterwards.

I was approaching my own thirteenth birthday in the February when I finally started full on puberty. I got my first hairs under my arms and around my groin, but to my dismay, Matt said that he preferred me smooth and shaved them every time we were together. Andy was allowed to grow his, but I wasn't. I think it was just another ploy of theirs to keep me as the "baby" of the group and be the submissive of them. After all, as I said before, while Andy was allowed to make love to me, I was never allowed to be the top with him. I was never allowed to top anyone, always being the bottom.

My parents never saw me naked after the age of ten so there was no fear of them seeing me, but I did get a lot of ribbing in the showers at school. One of the teachers even took me to one side at one point and explained that boys started puberty at different times and that

sometimes, boys didn't start until they were sixteen. Of course, I never told him that I had started but was being shaved because that would be telling on Matt, something that I'd never do.

The final piece of my submission came on Andys' fourteenth birthday. It had been some twenty months since I had first lost my virginity to him and Matt and I was basically now just going along with whatever they wanted. I'm not saying that I was a crushed soul, but I certainly was extremely submissive and compliant to them. Whatever Matt wanted to do with me, or to me, I'd let him if it meant getting to spend time alone with him.

If you don't want to read the next part, please skip ahead to the asterisks, as there will be explicit detail in this part. Why? Because again, it is something that has shaped my own sexual desires over the last four years since I met Tony. It is something that we have got very close to but never yet achieved.

It was half term, so again, we had gone to the cottage where Joe and George were waiting. The usual things happened, including that fingering had been introduced more and more. As I've mentioned, I have discovered that my hole is extremely sensitive and I did like it being played with and stretched… it was just the actual act of having the penises of men who weren't Matt inside me that I wasn't a great fan of.

It was the middle of the week and I had been played with a lot. We went into one of the bedrooms and I was put on my back, something I don't particularly like because it lets me see the man who was doing me, as well as that it sometimes meant that I didn't get my climax.

Each of them took their turn in doing it to me, my legs being held apart to allow them easier access. I know that I must have been complaining because I remember George telling me to quit or he'd put his underwear in my mouth. They did me twice each, climaxing inside me

each time, which made it not so bad as it was making my insides lubed up. That was what they had actually wanted.

The third time that Andy got in place, they stopped him and told him to put some lube on his fingers. He started pushing them into me, which I know that I must have liked, because I always did. What I wasn't prepared for was when he didn't stop at three or four fingers. I shouted out and tried to move but I was being held down and my legs were being held apart. Andy didn't stop until he had pushed his whole hand inside me. He moved it back and forth, and I remember that despite the pain, because he would have been pressing against my prostate, my dick was erect. They took turns sucking it while Andy moved his hand in and out and I had what I think must have been the most intense climax up to that point. I passed out and didn't wake up until the following morning wrapped in Matt's arms.

That opened up Andys' domination of me. For the next six weeks or so, he would do that to me and I know that he enjoyed it. While it did hurt, there was also a slight pleasurable side to it, something that I want desperately to replicate now that I am an adult. I do remember that Gerry also wanted to do it to me, but he couldn't get me to open up wide enough and Matt did step in and tell him to stop before he hurt me.

****

This is where you can start up reading if you skipped the last section.

It was about a month before Christmas when it all suddenly stopped. Matt announced that they were moving down south and that he would miss me and everything that we had been doing. They would be leaving within a couple of weeks and I cried into his chest as he held me that night.

The final time that we got together, it was just the three of us. Both of them made love to me all night, as we knew it would probably be the last time we ever saw each other. There were a lot of tears on my part, some on Andys' and a few on Matts', although looking back I'm not sure if they were tears that he'd miss me personally or just my body.

They left around two weeks before the end of term and it was the most miserable Christmas that I remember, even though my parents actually managed to get enough money together to buy me a pool table, not a proper one but it was still a full size six foot by three foot that we could put on top of the dining table.

Gerry did come to the school on the first Friday after I went back to school and I thought that maybe, just maybe, Matt and Andy were back. I got in the car with him but instead of going to a house, he drove us to a quiet lane. He started to grope me and wanted me to kiss him but I asked where the others were. He said that it was just him and asked if I wanted to have some fun. I didn't really want to but he said that he would leave me there if I didn't, so I said okay and he took down his trousers, made me get out of mine and he told me to sit on his penis. He made me kiss him when he did it but when it was over, I told him I wasn't interested in doing stuff with him anymore and that I only ever did it with him because Matt told me to. He said that "we'd see" but when he came around the following Friday, I had already made up my mind not to do it anymore. He tried to make me get in but when I started to make a fuss, he must have got worried about being in a public place and he left.

From that moment on, I never saw or heard from any of them again.

Andrew Michelson

Chapter Seventeen – Wednesday 7th October

Well I finally did it. Last night, I finally made contact and spoke with the male volunteer at the Rape and Sexual Violence Project. Funnily enough, I'd been for a couple of pints of Dutch courage straight from work and was just settling down on my sofa, having got washed and changed from my work clothes and had picked up my mobile to call them when it rang with a "No Caller ID" number. Guessing that it would be them, I answered, confident that I was ready to talk.

Of course, once he came on the phone, my nerves started but I did manage to get past them and made a joke about "how great minds think alike." That managed to get myself going and I explained that I wasn't sure what I wanted from the contact, that I had been sexually active as a twelve year old boy with men and that my initial and long term memories were that I had enjoyed it.

We spoke at length, for just under an hour, and while he was not judgemental, and said that it was going against his norm… but that if my over-riding memory was an enjoyable one, then I shouldn't allow other people to try to tell me how I should feel. I said to him that I feel like I should be very angry, because that is what society expects, but I just couldn't get to the levels that I thought were expected of me.

Having written to the point where Joe and George have been having sex with me, I do now feel some anger

towards how I was manipulated and coerced. Looking back, I can't help but argue with myself over Andy's involvement. He had certainly been groomed and used by the men, but he played a large role in my own grooming, but was he forced into it or did he do it knowing that he would also be able to have sex with me?

The project does offer a counselling service, but I need to be assessed before I can go so the man has put me forward onto the waiting list. Apparently it can take up to twelve weeks, just for the initial assessment. Worryingly for me, the assessment is with the chief counsellor who is a woman. Now, I don't mind explaining things to a man, especially if he has experience in dealing with men who have been abused but to try to explain to a woman why I liked it when a grown man penetrated my anus as a boy... that is completely different.

However, I did come off the phone feeling like a weight had been lifted slightly. I had finally gone into some detail about what had happened to me and tried to explain my feelings in a way that could be understood. And he did understand. Yes he had the underlying sentiments that, as a twelve year old, there was no way that I could give an informed consent to what was happening, but he did understand how I could have been led into believing that I was made to feel special by Matt and that I could have enjoyed certain aspects of the sex.

Looking back over the last chapter, I realise that there will be some people who will find the idea that a thirteen year old boy would allow himself to be fisted, or that it even could happen, is beyond their understanding. If the hole is prepared properly and the hand is small enough, then it will go in. Ever since I have met Tony, it is something that I have been desperate to try again. I must have gone through the entire collection on sites like Pornhub, but both Tony and James have so far only managed to get four fingers inside me. Tony got very

close, getting his hand to the knuckles before we had to stop but it is something that we have both promised we will achieve.

Having done a little research as to why men like being fisted, the explanation centres more on the handover of power by the bottom to the top during anal sex than the sex itself. After all, the top is the one who is penetrating the bottoms' anus with his penis while the bottom submits his body to the top for his use. The penis is the second most powerful icon of a man's body, behind the fist, so when it is the fist being used to penetrate, it is more powerful, more in control than ever. I think that because of how easily and how frequently I submitted myself to the five of them that has made me crave that handover more than most.

Anyway, while I await my assessment, and now that I have reached the point where I have been left alone by them, I will continue with the rest of my life, so to speak.

Andrew Michelson

Chapter Eighteen – Schooling and Beyond

After I went back to school following the Christmas break and had finally broken free of the attentions of Gerry, I had become depressed, alone, happy and frustrated all in one confused mix. I began acting out at school, becoming slightly rebellious to the point where I had stopped doing a lot of my homework. My grades were slipping and I was called into my Year Head's office to explain myself. I remember giving him attitude which landed me in detention and finally 'on report' due to missing so much homework. I was made to stand in front of my form class and explain what being 'on report' meant, which was basically having to take all of my school books to my form tutor twice a week for her to make sure that I was keeping up to date with my homework. I was put in permanent detention each break and lunchtime until I had caught up and the school report that term was a terrible one.

I had started to get stomach pains, which my GP put down to the stress that I was under at school and much to my embarrassment, for a time I began bedwetting again. I must have worried my parents senseless but, at the time, I didn't care. I think that the GP, my teachers and my parents put my problems down to my best friend of a year and a half suddenly leaving as well as the onset of puberty and teenage hormones. With Matt no longer

around, my underarm hair and my pubic hair were now growing as normal, something that the PE teacher had noticed and privately commented on to me.

Being in trouble at school actually helped me in a way as there were a couple of lads who previously hadn't really spoken to me who suddenly wanted to be friends. One of them, Paul, was from the next town which was mainly council properties and he became my new best friend. It seems strange how names work out. I had two best mates called Paul, and of course, Andy who was the same name as me. In the space of the next six months, I had more fights than I had in the whole of my school life so far.

As Paul was such a tough nut, I immediately tried to shun my sexuality. I still privately lusted after boys in my school, but I did manage to date a couple of girls.

There was Liz, who was the daughter of a friend of my Nan and Mum. Our families knew each other through the Guides and so, they were delighted when we started dating. I knew that my heart wasn't really in it, but we did manage to get caught in a quite heated make out session in her room. It was only kissing but it was obviously too much for her father and, after discussions with both parents, we cooled the action. In a way, I was probably quite pleased because if things had continued, we would probably have ended up having sex while we were still only fourteen and with no access to condoms, I may have become a teenage father. As the school year drew to an end, I sort of got bored of being with her, under the constant watch of her father, so I started to find excuses not to be with her to the point where she dumped me.

I thought that I would be free to finish the year off with my mates but literally the day after it got around that she'd dumped me, Jane was there. She was a girl in my form class, who had really big boobs, even at her age. I'd managed to avoid her attentions for a week or so but at

someones' birthday, we were playing Postmans' Knock and, unknown to me, it was fixed so that it was me and her outside in the hallway to kiss. I did my best with her but it was definitely lacking my previous attachments to Matt and Andy, so I must have put her off, thinking that I was a bit of a wet fish.

The second year finished, the third started and I knuckled back down to school work, improving my grades back to the levels that they were before. I never did get the courage to ask Paul if he wanted to play around at all, and so we went on to the Grammar School, where again, fate split me up from my best mate.

Just like the High School, the Grammar School had various feeder schools join them. There was four school years, the Fourth and Fifth years who were studying their GCEs, and the two years of the Sixth Form college who were doing their A' Levels. There must have been around two and a half thousand students easily, so again, the years were split in two. Paul was in one half and I was in the other.

Fortunately, this time, the form class was more like Primary School with the tables in a row, rather than individually placed. This allowed us to sit in groups and there were a few pupils that I knew from previous classes at the High School.

I think it was during my GCE's that I finally admitted to myself what I'd been hiding all along from everyone, and knew without doubt that I liked boys and men more than girls. I still didn't tell anyone, mainly due to a kid being beaten up for a rumour that he was gay. Fate, as always, placed me in situations that I both enjoyed and hated. There was a lad called Rob, who had been one of my crushes since the first year of High School and I found myself in three of his classes. We became friends, not best friends, but we did sit next to each other in all three classes. I found it difficult not to stare at him a lot. Other boys became fantasies again but I managed to

squirm my way through my GCEs, going on to Sixth Form college to do my A' Levels.

I had been accepted into Loughborough University, but when my results came through, I'd flunked a few of my exams, only getting one of the three grades needed and, not wanting to face a year of retakes, I found my first job at the age of eighteen.

I was working in a retail chain of shops, starting off as a YTS trainee in a shop surrounded by women. Normally, an eighteen year old boy would be delighted but I was still in hiding. I worked my way through the system, getting promoted to a team leader's role in a new superstore before being scouted to go to the head office in Yorkshire. This was a big move for me as it meant leaving home at the age of twenty two. It wasn't just moving out to my own place in my town, but was over a hundred miles away in Leeds, a large city where I would know absolutely no-one.

But I did it. I took the job but found myself in an environment where men were men. So again, I started dating women to hide my sexuality and went through a string of girlfriends, even having sex with a couple of them. To my shame and embarrassment, the first time that I tried, I couldn't keep an erection which I managed to bluff away that I had had too much to drink. The second time we tried it, I just imagined that I was with Matt and Andy and it seemed to work.

My job finished two years later when my company was bought out, and I moved back home. Jobs came and went for a time before I settled into one which kept me there for around seven years. During this time, I nearly came out several times to my best mates from the Grammar School who I had kept in touch with, but it was the landlady of my local pub who sussed me out. She was actually a lesbian herself, in a relationship and had a male friend who was also gay. He used to stay over

in the pub accommodation sometimes and I eventually admitted to them that I was gay.

One night, while Dave was looking after the pub, with the landlady and her partner away, I stayed behind to help him close up. I was a somewhat part-time barman for them. We finally made a move on each other and kissed in the bar after everyone had gone. I wanted to go upstairs to his room but he said that he was under threat of death that he couldn't have a man upstairs with him. I thought that was that, but he suggested that we could still do it but on the long, stretched sofa in the bar. I readily agreed, wanting, needed to have sex with a man once again. It had been fifteen years or so since that last night with Matt and Andy but I had been playing with myself throughout. Therefore it wasn't like I was a virgin all over again as he fingered me loose and penetrated me. God I loved it, the feeling when I was stretched open by him and with a request for him to masturbate me as I was on my hands and knees, doggy style, I climaxed with him inside me.

Unfortunately it was a one off thing, but it reminded me off the good times that I'd experienced with Matt and Andy.

I went back into my closet and stayed firmly there. I didn't date or anything until a girl that I remembered from a school year below me asked me out. To dispel any rumours about my sexuality, we dated and I found that she had two sons, both with different fathers. I actually knew one of them and it was a tense moment when I first bumped into him in the pub while I was dating the mother of his son. He soon put my mind at rest, telling me that he was engaged to another girl and that was that. I stopped over a couple of times, having sex with her, but she was a lot more sexually aggressive than I was expecting and I found myself unable to satisfy her demands. Our relationship lasted probably around

three months before we called it quits and parted as friends.

From then on, I kept my private life private. I would watch porn and hump my pillow as my only form of sexual relief but that all changed when the company that I worked for again was taken over, this time by a German company. I was in a buying role and when I was instructed to start using suppliers that I couldn't see any benefit to our UK branch, I started to question why. I found out that the German company was on kickbacks and I started to rebel, I guess. I constantly presented better, more competitive quotes from my previous suppliers and it was soon agreed that I would part ways with the company.

I started looking around once again, and eventually found employment with my current employer. Due to the location, which was around an hour and a half drive each way, I decided to move cities once again. I found a nice small village to live in and became friends with a good set of people.

I didn't date and, I found out later, that several rumours had gone around that people thought I must be gay. When I did come out to the friend who I had known the longest, his reaction was simply "yeah, me and the wife figured it out two years ago!" They were an exception to the rule as most of the people who now know, were surprised when I did tell them, as I am not camp or effeminate in any way.

From then on in, I came out to several other friends before settling into the comfortable routine that I wouldn't deny it if asked but I didn't shout it from the rooftops.

That's when one of my friends, who is also gay, told me about a hook up site. I tried it out and met Tony. That first meet. I will always remember it because I was nervous as hell. When he turned up, I nearly came there and then. He was everything that I had been wanting,

desiring. He is older than me by about ten years and, when asked, he can be very dominant. Our games in the bedroom have gone from just normal sex to the kinky role plays that both he and I liked, which is mainly the Dad/Son role plays that I mentioned previously.

I have had a few other one off meets, but Tony is my main guy. Unfortunately he is currently working a long way away so we haven't had a meet for some time. I recently met another guy called David, who I have mentioned before. He is sixty seven and is a big guy. He ticked all of my boxes on the first meet and, like Tony, I am desperate for another meeting with him.

All of my recent sexual encounters though have played out along similar lines. They are all with older men, they are all dominant men which allows my submissive side to come out and most of them are happy to have me face down on my bed while they hold me in place and use my body sexually. I have even replicated the encounters on the holidays by having meets that involve more than one partner and I let myself be taken by the group in turn.

All of this comes from what happened to me in the past, I am sure of it, but all of it, as an adult, is enjoyable and desired.

Andrew Michelson

Chapter Nineteen – In Conclusion

So here I am, almost at the end of my journey of rediscovery and remembrance. I was thinking about delaying until I had met with a counsellor, but with it a minimum of three months just for the initial assessment, I have decided to finish my story.

Looking back over the last two months, my attitude to my past has changed yet stayed the same, if that makes sense? I look back now, not realising at the time how young I was when I was first touched during that holiday with my Nan and Great Aunt. I look at it now and I am convinced that if I had gone back swimming the next day, then I would have been abused by Barry. Similarly, if I had been on my own at the phone booths, then I would probably have gone with the two men if they had asked me to. Who knows what they would have done?

There is always a big shout about the stranger danger situations, and it certainly did rear its head in my early life, but statistics show that the vast majority of child sexual abuse is carried out by adults known to the child, be them family members, friends of the family, or trusted adults such as scout leaders, teachers and of course, priests.

Mine fell into that latter category.

I still look back, reading through my journey, and cannot help but think about how fate placed me in that position, and about my own role in it. After all, it was me that instigated that first rape game with Andy, which

opened the door to him making more of a move on me. I sometimes wonder if Phil hadn't moved away, would he have been the target? Phil and Andy had been a lot closer than I was at the time, and Andy had been openly rubbing himself in front of him, but once he had gone, I was there to take his place.

The adult head in me knows that I am not to blame for anything, that the blame lies solely with the four men who used my young body, and Andys' body, in ways that shouldn't have happened. However, I do still place a small burden of guilt onto myself because what Matt did with me, I enjoyed it, at least once the initial discomfort had gone. I didn't like Joe and George and the things that I had to do with them, but even some of those were not bad. They made some of it fun, making some of it into a competition between Andy and myself, and I guess that I was just naïve enough to fall for it.

As I said to the male volunteer on the helpline, at the moment, I have no intention or desire to go to the police about what happened. Firstly, thinking about ages, the men will be at least late seventies if not into their eighties, unless of course they have already passed away. What point would there be in putting an eighty year old man in prison, other than to serve a need to punish the past?

Secondly, it would expose me to the greater world. It is one thing talking to the helpline, to a counsellor if it happens, to my fellow author and to Tony, but to have this exposed with my true name attached would be too much. It will become known to my parents, who I think would have their own guilt trips, as they practically forced me out of the door and into Matts' car to go on the holidays. If they ever found out what happened to me while I was there, I am sure that it would really hurt them that they didn't know or see what was happening.

Every day I walk to work. Every day, I pass the school children as the gather for the bus from our village to their schools in the town. Every day, I look at them and

wonder. If the statistics hold up, as I pass the sixty or so children, there are at least three currently being abused. There will be around six or seven boys who will be abused by the time they complete their GCSEs. I notice a couple of them who stand alone, not talking to any other child, but that isn't necessarily a sign. I spent eighteen months in the beds of the men who used my body for sex, yet I was still a happy go lucky boy who interacted with my peers. So every day, I wonder if any of them are going through what I went through, but are hiding it from the outside world.

So there it is. I still partially blame myself but know that it was mainly the fault of the men who took advantage of my crush on Matt and did some terrible yet pleasurable things to my body. They were the ones who have forged my adult desires to be dominated by older men and have them use my body for pleasure. They were the ones who took the innocence away from the twelve year old boy who trusted and loved Matt, only for him to betray me in the worst possible way.

When I get to go to the counselling, I will see if my confusion leads to the anger that I am supposed to feel towards Matt, and in a small part, Andy.

This has been a real challenge at times, to write and to re-live my past, but now that I am here, I am really pleased that I have done so. These are the experiences that shaped my life. Did I really enjoy what happened to me in the past? Or is it the rose tinted specs that can only remember the good and have blocked the bad? I will probably never really work it out in my head. Maybe if I am accepted in for counselling, then any hidden anger or emotions will come out, but until then, all I can do is tell it how it is and how it was.

This is my story.

Made in United States
North Haven, CT
28 August 2022

23365826R00093